COMPUTER DICTIONARY FOR BEGINNERS

COMPUTER DICTIONARY FOR BEGINNERS

Arthur Naiman

Ballantine Books • New York

This book was written on a microcomputer-based word processing system put together by Tony Pietsch. Built on an S-100 bus, it has a Z80 CPU running at 4MHz, 64K of RAM, two single-density 8" drives, and a NEC Spinwriter printer. The operating system is CP/M and the word processing program is WRITE; I also use The Word+ spelling checker.

Copyright © 1983 by Arthur Naiman

Illustrations on pp. 7, 30, 34, 42, 51, 55, 56, 73, 83, 84, 97, 110, 114, 125, 126, 128, 133, 138 Copyright © 1983 by Gar Smith

All rights reserved under International and Pan-American Copyright Conventions. Published in the United States by Ballantine Books, a division of Random House, Inc., New York, and simultaneously in Canada by Random House of Canada Limited, Toronto.
Some of the definitions in this book originally appeared in *Word Processing Buyer's Guide* by Arthur Naiman. Copyright © 1983 by McGraw-Hill, Inc.

Certain hardware and software products are mentioned by their trade names in this book. In most—if not all—cases these designations are claimed as trademarks by the respective companies. It is not our intent to use any of these names generically and the reader is cautioned to investigate all claimed trademark rights before using any of these names for any purpose other than to refer to the product described.

Library of Congress Catalog Card Number: 83-90068
ISBN: 0-345-31223-6

Manufactured in the United States of America

Designed by Gene Siegel

First Edition: October 1983

10 9 8 7 6 5 4 3 2 1

For R.
semper constans

Acknowledgments

It's every obsessive's dream to find someone who's as obsessive as s/he is, and about the same things. In my case, Ron Lichty answers that dream—at least as far as writing about computers is concerned. He was involved in every stage of this project and provided much crucial advice.

Like Ron, Tom Crosley read the manuscript at two different points and gave me the benefit of his expertise. Kevin Layer read a draft and critiqued it extensively; he caught several errors and provided a lot of important information. Stan Brenner also gave the manuscript a careful reading, and noticed some things everybody else missed.

I usually (but not always) followed the suggestions of these four computer experts. For that reason, and because there's so much I don't know about computers, I must place the responsibility for any errors which remain squarely on their shoulders.

Computer novices (or semi-novices) also read the manuscript and told me where it was unclear (or unfunny). Esther Wanning did that in addition to admirably performing her duties as my agent, which included endless hours of listening to my kvetching; Gloria Polanski did that in addition to helping me with the endless hassles of buying a house. Paul Glassner gave the manuscript a paricularly thorough and thoughtful going over. Meg Holmberg went through it twice and made many valuable recommendations. The diagram at **programming language,** the comparative illustrations at **motherboard** and **chip,** the special section on how computers work, and several other features of the book originated as her ideas.

Gar Smith produced more good cartoons than I could have hoped for, and put up with all my nit-picking to boot. Joelle Delbourgo showed the same exquisite taste in editing this book as she did in selecting it; I'm particularly grateful for her open-mindedness and reasonableness in discussions on various points. Ted Johnson did a superb job of copy editing.

I also want to thank the following people for support of many different kinds: Matthew Lasar, Tony Pietsch, Clem Cole, Sandy Van Broek, Guy Steele, Rita Gibian, Albert and Nettie Naiman, Stephen McNabb, Janet Pfunder, Jonathan Ayres, Cathy Roberts, Nancy Shine, Pat Diehl, Amy Bomse, Mark McDonald, Eric Jungerman, Burt Sloane, Richard Fateman, Margaret Butler, Ed Berman, Bill Hass, Debra Dadd, Phyllis Saifer, Gail Nielsen, Alan Levin, Miki Shima, Jane Margold, Ed Kelly, Brad Bunnin, Rose Slais, Ruth Anne Martin and Tom Brockland.

COMPUTER DICTIONARY FOR BEGINNERS

Introduction

At last—a dictionary of computer terms that isn't written for engineers. If you've been frustrated by computer jargon and haven't had any easy way to find out what it means, this book is for you.

Computer Dictionary for Beginners defines the 1100 or so terms you're most likely to come across when reading about computers, shopping for them, or trying to understand the manuals that come with them, and it explains those terms in clear, everyday, conversational English. There's even some humor (but never the kind that confuses you about the real meaning of a word).

Unlike other computer dictionaries, this book is designed for beginners. So I've kept technical terms out of the definitions as much as possible. The ones I do use are all defined elsewhere in the book; if you run across one that isn't familiar to you, it's easy to look it up.

Mostly I've chosen terms that refer to personal computers—the kind individuals can afford to buy and use themselves. I assume you're interested in *using* a computer, not in designing or building one, so engineering jargon like "virtual address" and "bit slice" is left out. But I have included some "hacker jargon"—the language computer experts use when talking to each other—not because you'll ever need to know it, but because it's interesting and fun.

Pronunciations are provided for all the terms that need them (including some you could find in a regular dictionary, if you went to the trouble). For many entries, the origins of the term are also given, as are typical sentences (in italics) to show how the term is used.

I've included several charts and diagrams, because certain information makes the most sense presented that way. Cartoons liven things up and help illustrate difficult concepts. A special section—*How Computers Work—in 500 Words or Less*—gives you a solid basic understanding that would be hard to get by looking up individual words.

If you come across a term you feel should be in this book but isn't, drop me a line at Ballantine Books, 201 East 50th Street, New York, New York 10022 and I'll try to include it in subsequent editions. But I think you'll find that just about any term you're likely to run into is already here.

How This Dictionary Works

Since I'm writing for nontechnical readers like yourself, I haven't tried to make my definitions more precise than you need them to be. Instead I've concentrated on making them clear and useful.

Some terms have applications wider than just computers, but I've only defined what they mean in the computer field. For example, the word "up" has dozens of meanings other than its computer meaning of "working."

Sometimes I've had to use technical terms in the definitions. If I hadn't, each definition would be ten pages long. But when I use a term that I think will be unfamiliar to most readers, I boldface it—so you know you can look it up (although, in fact, *all* the technical terms I use are defined elsewhere in the dictionary, whether they're boldfaced or not).

I also boldface synonyms for the word being defined, as well as additional words or phrases I'm defining at the same time (like **the field,** which means something different from the word **field** by itself).

Unless otherwise stated, abbreviations are pronounced letter by letter (for example, "EMI" is pronounced "ee-em-eye"). In the pronunciations, "g" is always hard (as in "go"); if I want to indicate soft "g," I use "j." By the same token, "s" always equals "ss," never "zz."

I haven't included brand names of popular programs or pieces of hardware, for two reasons:

1) what gets included and what gets left out of such a list is always subjective, and unfair to many excellent products an author simply doesn't know about; and

2) mentioning a brand name implies a certain sort of approval, and there are several popular products I wouldn't want anyone to think I endorse.

The exceptions to this rule are brand names that you're likely to come across in an ad for some other product, without any explanation as to what they are (like CP/M, SoftCard, and the names of various programming languages and CPU chips).

Some computer terms are numbers; for example, "8086" is the name of a type of chip. I list numbers in alphabetical order, mixed in with the other terms. Thus "8086" is under "e," because "eighty" begins with "e." But if there are several number terms right in a row, I put them in ascending numerical order, rather than in strict alphabetical order.

I alphabetize as if each entry were one long word; spaces and hyphens don't count. Symbols are listed at the end of the book. Terms that begin with a symbol but also include letters (like **.TXT** and **/bin**) are listed by their first letter.

How Computers Work—in 500 Words or Less

I won't waste any words telling you that 500 words isn't going to allow for a very detailed picture of how . . . oh my God! I've just wasted 28 . . . no, 30 . . . uh . . .

Look at the drawing below. All computers (and word processors) are made up of these basic pieces of **hardware** (some

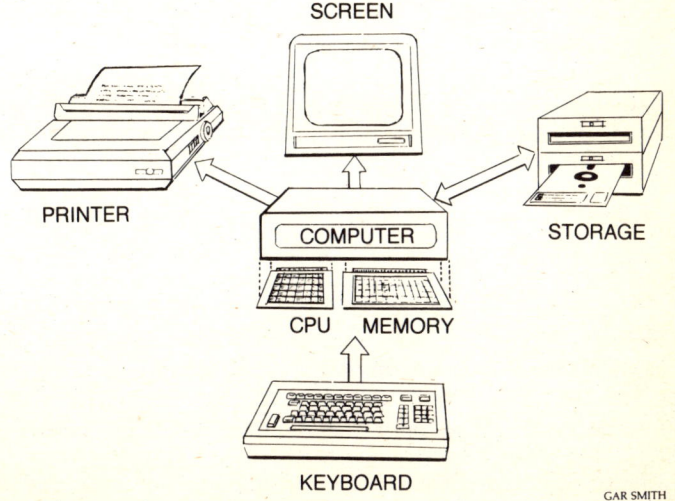

include other components too, of course). When you type a character (any letter, number or symbol) on the keyboard, a coded electronic impulse travels over a cable to the computer, where it's stored in **memory** (this kind of memory is called **RAM**).

A computer's memory is basically a whole slew of little switches. Since a switch can only be on or off, computers reduce all information to a series of ons and offs, ones and zeros (in much the same way that Morse Code reduces all communications to a series of dots and dashes).

Today's computer technology allows thousands of electronic switches to be squeezed onto a piece of silicon the size of a baby's fingernail (called a **chip**). These chips are mounted and wired together on thin slabs of fiberglass called **boards**.

Not only are the switches used in computers very small, they're also very fast; some computers can throw millions of switches a second. (Primitive computers used mechanical switches, which were relatively big, clumsy and slow.)

Once a character is lodged in RAM, it's transmitted to a screen much like the one on your TV, which is also called a **monitor** or **display**. (Did you notice how I saved a word back there by using "it's" instead of "it is"?)

To actually *do* something to the characters you've placed in RAM—that is, to process your data—you need the **CPU** (the "central processing unit"). The CPU—made up of one or more chips—is capable of doing thousands of calculations a second; whatever a computer does, from word processing to Donkey Kong, it reduces to numerical calculations (to switch-throwing, really).

When you turn your computer off, RAM goes blank, so you need some way to permanently store your processed data (whether it's a letter, a game you've written, or a list of your accounts receivable). This is done on a **storage device** which puts your information on **media** like **floppy disks, hard disks** or cassette tapes; these store data in the form of magnetic impulses—basically the same way recording tapes store sound.

Another use for storage devices is to "load" **software** (instructions to the computer—also called **programs**) into the computer. These instructions can also be given to a computer by a special kind of hard-to-change memory called **ROM**, but programs on disks are usually more convenient (because you can change them much more quickly).

Since shipping your whole computer system to someone is a little inconvenient, **printers** were invented to produce **hard**

copies (on paper) of letters or other documents. It's also convenient to have hard copies for your own use, because it gets to be annoying to always have to look at things on the screen.

498 . . . 499 . . . I did it!!! . . . whoops.

Dictionary

A

A: In **CP/M, PC DOS** and some other **operating systems,** this means "(disk) drive A."

ABC The "Atanasoff-Berry computer"—an early electronic computer built in 1942 by John V. Atanasoff and Clifford Berry. That and earlier work by Atanasoff were used to break the patent of Mauchly and Eckert (inventors of **ENIAC** and **UNIVAC**) on the basic technology used in all electronic digital computers. (Honeywell sued, claiming that Eckert and Mauchly had "pirated" their ideas from Atanasoff.)

-AC Abbreviation for "automatic computer," much used as the last two letters of computer names in the '40s and early '50s. The "automatic" distinguishes computing machines from somebody with a slide rule and a pencil, who could (back then) conceivably be called a "computer."

(to) access To get to; to avail oneself of the contents of. A more specific meaning is to transfer data to or from a storage device (or memory). *WordStar is slow because it's always accessing the disk.*

access time How long it takes to put data onto—or take data off of—a storage device (or into and out of memory).

acoustic coupler A **modem** you put the handset of a telephone in. Its microphone picks up the incoming sound signals from the telephone's earpiece; its speaker sends outgoing sound signals, generated by the computer, into the telephone's mouthpiece. As opposed to **direct-connect modems** that plug right into the phone jack.

Ada (AY-duh) A **high-level programming language** developed for the U.S. Department of Defense and introduced in the early 1980s. Based on **Pascal** but much more complex, Ada is supposed to be the DOD's standard language into the next century, but many doubt it will last that long.

Ada is named after Ada **Lovelace,** one of the more romantic figures in the history of computing.

address A number that tells the computer where in memory a piece of data is stored.

addressable cursor A **cursor** you can move all over the screen (as opposed to one that will only move right and down, for example). Also called a **controllable cursor.**

address bus The part of the **bus** that carries the **address.** Distinguished from the **data bus.**

AI Abbreviation for **artificial intelligence.**

ALGOL (AL-gawl) A **high-level programming language** introduced around 1960, designed for scientific applications. It's more popular in Europe than in the United States. The name comes from *"algo*rithmic *l*anguage" and usually has a suffix after it that indicates the version: ALGOL60, ALGOL-W, ALGOL68, etc.

algorithm (AL-guh-ri-thum) The precise sequence of steps required to do something. To program, you first figure out the algorithm, then turn it into a flow chart, then write **code** (a really hot programmer can eliminate the middle step). See **flowchart** for examples of all three steps.

Algorithms are usually not written down (except as actual code); it's just thinking them through that's important. *These two programs accomplish the same end, but they use different algorithms to do it.*

alphanumeric (AL-fuh-noo-MARE-ik) Composed of letters,

numbers and symbols like . and -. All text is alphanumeric, but many other kinds of data are only numeric.

alpha testing Trying a new product out on the employees of your own company. Compare **beta testing**.

ambient temperature How hot or cold the air is around a piece of equipment (which can affect its performance).

analog Continuous; not broken up into little pieces. Opposite of **digital**.

An analog computer compares actual physical things—like distances, electrical resistances or voltages—with each other, without breaking them up into little pieces, while a digital computer reduces everything to numbers and compares those. See **digital** for a fuller explanation.

The name "analog" comes from the fact that an analogy is being made between two physical things.

analytical engine See Charles **Babbage**.

ANSI (AN-SEE) The American National Standards Institute—a nonprofit federation of standards-writing organizations. ANSI keeps records of tens of thousands of voluntary standards in many different fields, including all aspects of computing.

There is, for example, an ANSI standard for **BASIC**. It specifies which commands should be included—as a minimum—in any language that gets called BASIC (there are some versions of BASIC that are a little *too* basic). Also see **ISO**.

APL A **high-level programming language** developed by Iverson and Falkoff at IBM and used mostly in statistical applications. The name stands for "a programming language."

Apple DOS The **operating system** used on Apple IIs. Apple itself usually calls it simply **DOS**.

applications programs (or **applications software**) Programs that do jobs (like word processing or accounting) which are relatively complicated, practical and specific. Distinguished from **systems software, learning programs** and games. Also see the diagram and explanation at **programming language.**

architecture The design of a computer system or component;

the way the parts that make it up are arranged and interrelate. *The architecture of the Z80 chip is similar to that of the 8080.*

(to) **archive** A synonym for **save,** used mostly on **dedicated word processors.**

"Archiving" is sometimes also used to refer to long-term storage, as opposed to "backing-up," which implies short-term storage.

(the) **ARPAnet** (ARP-uh-net) A government computer network that links Department of Defense sites like SAC headquarters and the Ames Research Center with most of the major computer think tanks (at places like Stanford, MIT, Carnegie-Mellon and the RAND Corporation). On the positive side, the famed **Jargon File** can be accessed on the ARPAnet. The name comes from the Advanced Research Projects Agency.

array Any sequential arrangement of items. A table of numbers in columns and rows is one kind of array.

artificial intelligence The branch of computer science that works on getting computers to think like human beings. The basic distinction between AI and other kinds of programming is that AI programs can *learn* from their own mistakes and can modify themselves so that they won't make the same mistakes again. Thus the AI programs that play chess keep getting better (they're already better than you).

Some typical AI concerns—aside from game-playing—are communicating in **natural languages** (like English) and proving mathematical theorems. Virtually all AI programming is done in **LISP.** Also see **Fredkin prize** and **Turing test.**

ASCII (ASK-ee) The most common code used for transmitting text between computers, or between a computer and its **peripherals.** Each letter, number and symbol has its own numerical equivalent in ASCII's **binary** code. Thus a capital "A" is 01000001 in ASCII; a lowercase "a" is 01100001; and so on.

"ASCII" stands for "American standard code for information interchange."

assembler A computer program that takes the programmer's **assembly language** statements and turns them into **machine language,** so the computer can execute them.

See the diagram and explanation at **programming language**.

assembly (or **assembler**) **language** Programming languages that talk fairly directly to the computer. Unlike **machine language** (which is what the computer understands), assembly language is **mnemonic,** so that it can be understood and remembered more easily by a human being; in fact, assembly language is really just machine language in mnemonic form. Also distinguished from **high-level languages** (which are farther away from machine language and closer to human speech).

Assembly languages are specific to a given **CPU chip** and are named after it (e.g., 8080 assembly language, 6809 assembly language, etc.). Assembly language is harder to program in than a high-level language, but it produces programs that are more efficient and run faster (in the hands of a competent programmer).

See the diagram and explanation at **programming language**.

asynchronous or **async** (ay-SING-krun-us; AY-sink) Not synchronized; not happening at regular time intervals.

In the **asynchronous transmission** of data, the time between each character varies; therefore each character has to be introduced with a **bit** or two of information that means "start" (to get the receiving end ready) and ended with a bit or two that means "stop" (so the receiving end knows that this little piece of the transmission has ended).

Since it has to go to all this trouble, asynchronous transmission is naturally less efficient than **synchronous** transmission. Also see **handshaking.**

auto-answer A feature of some **modems.** It means that they can automatically answer incoming phone calls (from other computers) and pipe the data from them into your computer.

auto-repeat A feature of some keyboards. Auto-repeat means that when you hold down a key, it will automatically—and rapidly—repeat. A delay (usually about half a second) is built in, to minimize accidental repeats.

auxiliary memory Another name for **storage.** Also called **auxiliary storage.**

"Auxiliary" is used here as the opposite of "main" (memory or storage). See **memory** for more on this morass of conflicting terminology.

B

B: In **CP/M, PC DOS** and some other **operating systems,** this means "(disk) drive B."

Babbage, Charles (1792–1871) Not a character out of Dickens, as his name might lead you to suspect, but a British mathematician who invented the "difference engine" (which could calculate logarithms to twenty decimal places) and the "analytical engine" (the first machine designed to process information in basically the same way computers do today).

COURTESY OF INTERNATIONAL BUSINESS MACHINES CORPORATION

The machinists of Babbage's time couldn't produce parts precise enough to make the analytical engine run, but his design was perfectly sound; in fact, a working model of the analytical engine was subsequently built—in the 20th century. Thus Babbage has as much claim as anyone to the title "inventor of the computer."

In addition to his work with computers, Babbage created the first reliable actuarial tables, invented the speedometer, the cowcatcher and the skeleton key, and demonstrated that a flat fee for postage produced greater revenues than fees based on distance. Also see Ada **Lovelace.**

Babbage's Difference Engine   COURTESY OF INTERNATIONAL BUSINESS MACHINES CORPORATION

Baby Blue A **board** that plugs into the IBM Personal Computer and allows it to run **CP/M-80,** by **slaving** the PC's own 8088 **CPU chip** to the Z80 chip on Baby Blue. Also see **SoftCard.**

background Anywhere outside of a computer's main focus of interest (which is relating to you). A **background program** runs unattended at the same time the computer is interacting with you to do some other job. Printing out one file while you're editing another is called **background printing.**

backplane Another name for a **motherboard.**

backslash A special computer character (\) which is never found in normal text and is therefore useful for distinguishing commands.

backup (file or **disk)** An extra copy, kept in case the original is harmed or destroyed.

bagbiting {hacker jargon} Worthless. *This bagbiting system is* *wedged again.* In tone, "bagbiting" is almost an obscenity. See **bogus** for a list of synonyms.

Can also be separated into a noun and verb: *Their new terminal really bites the bag.* Also see **chomp**.

.BAK (dot-BACK) In **CP/M**, a common **file type** used to identify backup files.

bang {hacker jargon} A spoken abbreviation for "exclamation mark." Useful when proofreading: *Quote take your hand off my knee bang endquote shrieked the duchess period.*
Excl and **wow** are also used.

bank switching The ability of some computers to switch between large chunks of memory. For example, **eight-bit chips** can only **address** 64K of memory directly; thus eight-bit computers that have more than 64K of memory must use some type of bank switching.

barfulous {hacker jargon} Said of something so bad it makes you want to barf (throw up). *CP/M documentation is absolutely barfulous.* **Barfucious** is also used. See **bogus** for a list of synonyms.

BASIC A **high-level programming language,** very popular on microcomputers, developed by Kemeny and Kurtz at Dartmouth College around 1973. There are many different dialects and brands of BASIC; **MBASIC** and **CBASIC** are two of the most popular.

BASIC is called a **low-level language** by some because it lacks certain features of more powerful high-level languages.

"BASIC" stands for "beginners all-purpose symbolic instruction code"—although I bet the acronym came first and the full name only later, as a rationale for it.

batch processing A mode of computer operation in which there's no immediate interaction between the user and the machine. Programs to be executed are collected together into prioritized batches (**queues,** in other words) and then run; the results are returned to the user when the computer gets around to it. Opposite of **interactive** or **real-time** processing.

baud rate (bawd) The number of bits per second. Baud rates are most commonly used as a measure of how fast data is transmitted—by a **modem,** for example. Named after Baudot, who devised a pre-**ASCII** communications code.

(In some circumstances there is a difference between bits per second and the baud rate, but for all practical purposes you can consider them to be the same.)

Baud rates can mean the difference between sanity and three weeks in Bellevue. If you can stand to watch text come onto a screen at 300 baud, you either have no central nervous system or you're the Buddha. 9600 baud begins to be reasonable and 19,200 is a real delight.

BBN Bolt Beranek and Newman—a private computer think tank located in Cambridge, Massachusetts (it designed the **ARPAnet** and was involved in some of the early development of **LOGO**).

bcnu {hacker jargon} An abbreviation for "be seein' you"—widely used to terminate typed conversations on computer terminals.

BDOS (BEE-doss) In **CP/M** and some other **operating systems,** the part of the program that customizes it to your particular disk drives. The name stands for "basic disk operating system." Most users of CP/M are more familiar than they'd like to be with **BDOS errors,** which look something like this when they appear on the screen: BDOS ERROR ON A: R/O (which means that the operating system can't read disk A for some reason, but hasn't tried to write to it). Compare **BIOS.**

Bell Labs The phone company's huge network of research facilities, which sometimes do work that has little to do—at least directly—with telephones. (As you may know, Ma Bell used to be the nation's largest weapons contractor.) The Bell Lab at Murray Hill, New Jersey—where the transistor was invented and **UNIX** developed—is one of the leading computer research centers in the country (among other things).

bells and whistles {hacker jargon} Features of a product which are likely to appeal to someone thinking of buying it, but which aren't essential to its operation. *The program's basically written; all we're doing now is adding some bells and whistles.*

benchmark A standard test, used to measure the efficiency of a computer or other device. Often a benchmark is a program that runs a computer through a series of tasks like adding 1 + 2, then 1 + 2 + 3, then 1 + 2 + 3 + 4, and so on up to a billion or so (isn't it lucky computers don't get bored?).

beta testing Having people who don't work for your company (such as business associates, friends, etc.) try a new product out. If a company is large, testing a product in another division or group from the one that developed it is sometimes also called beta testing. Compare **alpha testing**.

bi-directional Refers to printers that print one line from the left to right, the next from the right to left, and so on. This eliminates carriage returns, speeds up the printout, and looks amazing.

Sometimes "bi-directional" is also used to refer to **full duplex** transmissions.

bin On a **cut-sheet feeder,** a tray that holds blank paper or envelopes.

.BIN (dot-BIN) A common **file type** used to identify **binary files.** Also see **.COM**.

/bin (slash-BIN, or just BIN) In **UNIX** and some other operating systems, a common name for the **directory** that contains the system commands.

binary file A file containing **machine language** code, meant to be executed as a program (as opposed to a **data file** or a program in **source code** that you're working on).

binary numbers The numbers computers themselves understand. Composed entirely of zeros and ones, they express all values in powers of two (for those of you raised on the New Math, in base two).

You don't actually need to know much about binary numbers to use a computer, but let me explain a little about them anyway, just so you won't wince every time you hear the term.

The advantage of the binary system is that you only need two symbols (0 and 1) to express any number, no matter how big it is. Since computers are basically just large groups of switches, and since these switches can only be either on or off, binary fits right in; you just define 0 as "off" and 1 as "on" and then binary numbers tell the computer which switches to throw.

Here's a list of the (decimal) numbers zero through fifteen, with their equivalents in binary notation:

```
0 =  0      4 = 100      8 = 1000     12 = 1100
1 =  1      5 = 101      9 = 1001     13 = 1101
2 = 10      6 = 110     10 = 1010     14 = 1110
3 = 11      7 = 111     11 = 1011     15 = 1111
```

(*Why* those are the equivalents is an interesting story, but one there isn't room enough to go into here.)

BIOS (BYE-ohss) In **CP/M** and some other **operating systems,** the part of the program that customizes it to your computer. The name stands for "basic input/output system." Compare **BDOS.**

bisynchronous or **bisync** (bye-SING-krun-us; BYE-sink) A type of **synchronous** data transmission where the timing is controlled by signals generated at both the receiving and sending end. Used on IBM's popular 3270 line of terminals.

bit The smallest possible unit of information. All a bit can say is yes or no, on or off, or—as it's expressed in binary numbers—0 or 1. Short for *"binary digit"*. Also see **byte.**

bit decay {hacker jargon} A mythical disease of software. See **software rot.**

bit-mapped display A type of **memory-mapped video** where every **pixel** on the screen has a corresponding bit in memory. When memory changes, so does the display—instantly. Used on the Apple Lisa and other systems. Compare **terminal mode.**

bletcherous (BLEH-chur-us) {hacker jargon} Disgusting, worthless (from **bletch,** a term of disgust). See **bogus** for a list of synonyms.

block A unit of measure for how much **memory** or **storage** space a file takes up. Blocks often consist of 256 or 512 **bytes.**

In phrases like **block moves** and **block operations,** "block" doesn't refer to any specific amount of text; it's just used as a synonym for "chunk" or "piece."

block moves In word processing, the electronic equivalent of **cut & paste.** A block moves feature allows you to mark a block of text and move it anywhere you want in a file.

It's also possible to **block copy** (the block stays in its original position, in addition to appearing in the new place) and **block delete**. The generic name for all three is **block operations**.

(to) **blt** (blit) {hacker jargon} To transfer a large chunk of information from one place to another. The name comes from a command on the **PDP-10** and is short for "*bl*ock *t*ransfer."

board A piece of fiberglass or pressboard on which **chips** are mounted. The connections between the chips can be wires, or can be printed with metallic ink on the board (in which case it's a **printed circuit board**). Also called a **card**.

Boards are mounted inside the computer, and often inside **peripherals** and other devices. There are lots of different kinds of boards—memory boards, video boards, CPU boards, I/O boards and so on. Also see **chip**.

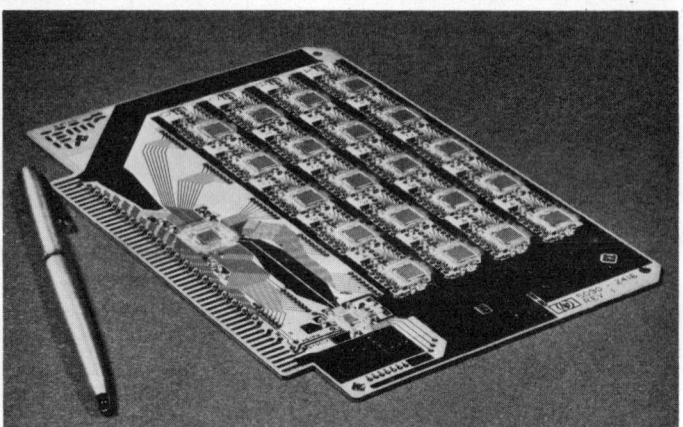

a board COURTESY OF HEWLETT-PACKARD

bogometer (bo-GAH-muh-ter) {hacker jargon} A mythical device for detecting **bogosity**. *When he started talking about the company's dedication to this project, my bogometer went berserk.*

bogosity (bo-GAH-si-tee) {hacker jargon} Phoniness; incorrectness; uselessness; stupidity. From **bogus**.

bogus {hacker jargon} Fake; wrong; useless; stupid.

Hacker jargon is rich in words meaning "worthless" or

"no good." The reason for this is fairly obvious, but I'll explain it anyway:

Groups of people coin words for things in their environment that are important to their survival. Thus Eskimos have fourteen words for different kinds of snow and only one for anything that flies (be it an insect, a bird or an airplane)—because snow is important to their survival and things that fly aren't.

In the same way, bogus equipment and software are major factors in making hackers happy or miserable. To maintain their sanity, hackers need a rich, full range of terms with which to heap abuse on the brain-damaged, bagbiting crud that can make their lives so difficult.

Below is a list of just a few of the most common of these terms. (For some obscure reason, many of them begin with a b, and they tend to cluster near the start of the alphabet.) All of these terms share the common meaning of "no good." Subtle distinctions in their use are indicated in parentheses.

bagbiting (almost an obscenity)
barfulous (can be used to refer to something which works OK but is ugly or clumsy)
bletcherous (a slightly humorous term)
bogus (the basic term)
brain-damaged (said of something so screwed up that it's hard to figure out what the people responsible for it imagined they were doing)
chomping (similar to bagbiting, but milder in tone)
cretinous (usually refers to people)
crufty (poorly built and/or physically disgusting, especially to the touch)
demented (usually refers to a program that works as designed, but was designed wrong)
fried (not working because of hardware failure; also said of people who are burned out, exhausted)
losing (a general term for anything that fails)
random (has the sense of "typically worthless")

boilerplate Pieces of text that get used over and over again, word for word, in different documents. Here's an example everybody's familiar with: *Your mileage may vary. Highway mileage will probably be lower.*

(Did you ever stop to think how many hours and dollars that could otherwise be put to productive use are wasted by writing, reading, airing and listening to that ridiculous disclaimer? What could all that time and effort produce *instead*, if Detroit let the EPA set up a realistic mileage test?)

boldfacing A feature of some printers and word processing programs which lets them imitate the look of a boldface type font ("**computer boldfacing looks like this**"). On many computer printers, boldfacing is produced by **shadow printing.**

Boole, George (1815–64) British mathematician and inventor of the mathematical logic (called **Boolean algebra**) which was later used as the basis for the design of computer circuits.

(to) boot To start up a computer by **loading** the **operating system** into it.

Also used as a noun. If you're just turning the system on, it's a **cold boot.** If you dump what you've been working on and reload the operating system, it's called a **warm boot,** or **rebooting.** On some IBM equipment, the acronym **IPL** (for "initial program load") is used. Also see **reset** and **system reset.**

The name comes from the idea that the operating system pulls the computer up by its bootstraps (you load a program that tells the computer how to load other programs).

bound Limited by. *The speed of this subroutine is bound by the time it takes to rewrite the screen.* Also see **I/O-bound** and **processor-bound.**

box The case a computer comes in (not the packing crate, but the actual cabinet)—but only if the keyboard is separate

a typical computer box COURTESY OF MORROW DESIGNS

from it. (If the keyboard isn't separate, there is no special name for the keyboard/box combination; it's simply called "the computer.")

In addition to enclosing the computer, the box also contains the **motherboard**, the **bus** and the **power supply.** *They make a nice box—it can really handle power surges. Unfortunately, their keyboard is absolute junk.*

The term "box" is also used to include the boards and other components inside the case—that is, what you'd normally just call the computer (here again, only when the keyboard isn't integral). *The system comes in four pieces—the monitor, the printer, the keyboard and the box.* Also called a **mainframe.**

bpi "Bits per inch"—a measure of the density with which information is recorded on **magnetic media.**

bps "Bits per second"—a measure of the speed at which data is transmitted. Also see **baud rate.**

brain-damaged {hacker jargon} Completely unusable due to idiotically bad design. See **bogus** for a list of synonyms.

breadboard A first rough model or prototype of a new circuit. The name goes back to the days when electronic hobbyists used their mothers' or wives' breadboards to build radios on.

broken {hacker jargon} When said of programs, not working properly. When said of people, it means more or less the same thing—acting strange or depressed.

btw {hacker jargon} An abbreviation for "by the way"—widely used to save time and effort in typed conversations on computer terminals. Sometimes written as **obtw** ("oh, by the way").

bubble memory An advanced—and expensive—kind of **storage.** Although it comes on a **board** and in the form of chips (of a sort), it stores data magnetically, not electronically. Bubble memory features high concentration and fast transfer of information.

buffer A hunk of **memory** set aside to hold data temporarily. It's often used to compensate for the fact that different devices operate at different speeds. So, for example, a printer—which is much slower than a computer—may have a buffer to hold data fed to it by the computer.

In word processing, the **workspace** you write in is also called a buffer. (In this case, the slower device is you.)

bug A mistake in a piece of software (or, less frequently, hardware).

Most computer programs are so complex that no programmer can test out (or even conceive of) all the possible situations they can generate. Thus most bugs aren't quite errors, but are rather untested paths, unanticipated contingencies. They're discovered when a user breaks new ground—for example, by using a particular series of commands in a particular order that no one has tried before.

"Bug" is an old electronics and phone company term. It comes from the humorous explanation for a problem "Bugs ate the insulation off the wires." In fact, this was the actual cause of many problems with early phone systems, until they figured out how to coat wires with stuff that bugs don't like the taste of.

Also see **feature** and **misfeature**.

bulk storage Another name for **storage,** although it can also refer to storing *huge* quantities of information — **gigabytes** and beyond.

bulletin board See **electronic bulletin board.**

bundled Sold together as one package, so that you can't buy the individual pieces. Whole systems are often bundled, as are groups of related programs. As opposed to **unbundled.**

burn-in period The first week or 200 hours of a computer's (or a component's) life, during which time it's much more likely to fail than later on (the computer equivalent to infant mortality).

To burn something in, manufacturers just turn it on and leave it on for the burn-in period. (Sometimes they also raise the **ambient temperature,** or cycle it up and down.)

Some manufacturers burn in their hardware for you. (If they don't, you do it yourself ... as you use it.) Once something has been burned in, you can usually depend on it for a while.

burst speed The top speed of a printer, which on **formed-character printers** is usually the speed at which it can repeatedly print one letter.

bus Circuits that connect the **CPU** with the **memory, I/O**

boards, and other devices in a computer (called the "bus" because they transport information around). The bus connects all the slots of the **motherboard**. It's composed of two parts: the **address bus** and the **data bus**.

While many microcomputers are designed with their own proprietary buses, there are also buses that have been standardized among manufacturers. The most common of these is the **S-100 bus**.

byte Eight **bits**—the amount of information required to define one character. (Bytes are also used in nontextual data that doesn't contain characters.) Also see **kilobyte**.

C

C A **high-level programming language** developed at Bell Labs and associated with the **UNIX** operating system. It's called C simply because it's an enhancement of an earlier language called B (which in turn was an enhancement of A).

CAD "Computer-aided design"—using computers to design something, usually a machine.

CAI "Computer-assisted instruction"—using computers to teach something.

CAM "Computer-aided manufacturing"—using computers to control a manufacturing process.

canned software Programs written by someone else that you buy and use. As opposed to **custom software**.

canonical {hacker jargon} Typical; standard—as used by hackers, that is. Thus the canonical meaning of **dragon** is not "giant, fire-breathing lizard," but rather "subservient program." (By the same token, "pertaining to church law" is not the canonical meaning of "canonical," because that isn't the way *hackers* use the word.)

card Another name for a **board**. Sometimes "card" also refers to a **punched card**.

card cage Another name for a **motherboard**.

carriage return A command and/or symbol that moves the **cursor** (or the printout) to the start of the line.

The important thing to remember is that—unlike the situation on a typewriter—just a carriage return doesn't move you down a line. For that, you need a **carriage return/line feed,** which—as its name implies—combines those two functions. (Just to make it more confusing, people often refer to a carriage return/line feed simply as a carriage return.)

The usual abbreviations are **cr, crlf** (for carriage return/line feed, of course) and **RETURN** (all caps)—because that's how the key is labeled on most keyboards. Also see **line feed**.

CAT "Computer-aided training"—using a computer to teach somebody how to do something.

A CAT is also a device on some Xerox keyboards that's used to move the **cursor** around. (I'd tell you what it stands for but the PR guy at Xerox didn't know himself.) Obviously it's a play on **mouse** (which is a cursor-movement device that's detached from the keyboard). Also see **rotary control knob** and **trackball**.

catalog In some **operating systems,** a list of all the files on a disk. More commonly called a **directory** (so you have the choice of imagining yourself leafing through brightly colored pages or standing in the lobby of an office building looking at the wall), although "directory" doesn't necessarily imply a list of *all* the files.

catatonic {hacker jargon} Said of a system or program that's locked up, stuck, unable to proceed without outside intervention. Sometimes due to a **deadlock**. Also called **wedged**.

CBASIC (SEE BAY-sic) A version of BASIC published by Digital Research. The "C" stands for "compiled," because CBASIC—unlike most versions of the language—is **compiled** rather than **interpreted**.

Centronics (or **Centronics-type**) **interface** A standard kind of **parallel interface,** originally used to connect Centronics (brand) printers with computers.

(to) chain Commonly used to mean "connect" or "link." For example, you can chain **records** together.

chain printer A kind of high-speed printer that uses a revolving chain on which slugs with characters on them are mounted. The chain moves the characters in front of the hammers that knock them into the paper. Chain printers make a *lot* of noise, but most of them are really fast.

character The generic name for a letter, number or symbol.

character buffer On a printer, a **buffer** the computer pumps text into, so it doesn't have to wait until all the text is printed out before it's free to deal with other jobs.

On a terminal, the character buffer is where data is sent before being displayed on the screen—usually so the terminal can **format** it.

character set All the characters a particular terminal, printer, **daisy wheel** or other device is capable of producing.

Also—all the characters a particular coding system is capable of recognizing (e.g., the ASCII character set).

character string See **string.**

chip Silicon is a chemical element found in sand, clay, glass, pottery, concrete, brick, etc. A piece of silicon (or of **germanium**) about the size of a baby's fingernail is impregnated with impurities in a pattern that creates different kinds of miniaturized computer circuits. This is a chip. Chips can contain the equivalent of hundreds or thousands of transistors, which makes them about the most impressive thing you can do with sand.

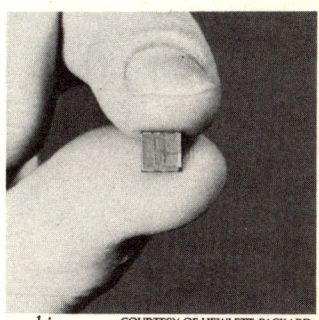
a chip COURTESY OF HEWLETT-PACKARD

"Chip" is also used more loosely to refer to the package in which the chip is contained (usually a **DIP**). In computers, chips (in their DIPs) are almost always mounted onto **boards,** where they do computations, remember data, etc.

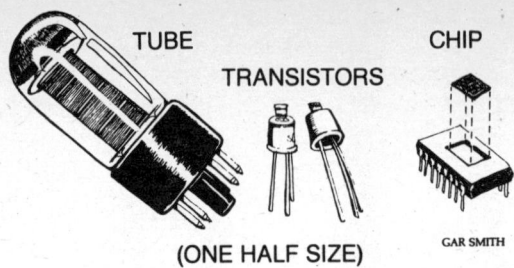

(ONE HALF SIZE)

Chips are also called **integrated circuits** or **ICs**. Integrated circuits were developed at more or less the same time by several different people, but the major credit is usually given to Robert Noyce of Fairchild Semiconductor and Jack Kilby of Texas Instruments.

one chip (foreground) can contain the equivalent of half-a-million transistors (background)   COURTESY OF HEWLETT-PACKARD

Whole **mainframe** computers have been reduced to a chip (that is, the computing part of them—the **CPU**—has; lots of other devices are required before the CPU can do anything useful, like remember the results of its calculations). Hewlett-Packard talks about a chip of theirs being "faster than a speeding bullet." A quarter-inch on a side, it can perform 500 operations in the time it takes a bullet to travel across it.

Chips are distinguished by how much circuitry is in them. The chart below gives you the various categories:

Categories of chips

Abbreviation	What abbreviation stands for	Equivalent of about how many switches (transistors) it contains
SSI	small-scale integration	up to 100
MSI	medium-scale integration	100-1000
LSI	large-scale integration	1000-50,000
VLSI	very-large-scale integration	50,000+

chip family A group of related chips, each of which (except the first) evolved from an earlier chip in the family. Usually all the chips in a family are made by the same manufacturer, but not always.

(to) chomp {hacker jargon} To fail; to be no good. *This new editor really chomps.* (The word probably comes from **bagbiter,** since "to chomp" means the same as "to bite the bag.")

A **chomper** is a loser. **Chomp chomp** is also used, either by itself or to intensify another word. *What a bagbiter! Chomp chomp.* There's also a gesture that means "chomp chomp"— the thumb acts as the lower jaw, the other four fingers as the upper jaw, and you make a series of rapid biting motions (similar to the common gesture that means "all s/he does is talk, talk, talk").

clock *Not* what it normally means (although the meaning is related). A computer's clock sends out electronic pulses that are used to synchronize the various things the computer does.

The **clock rate** is the speed at which these pulses are generated, and is measured in **megahertz** (MHz). Also see **real-time clock.**

(to) close (a file) To make it inaccessible to, or to release it from, a particular program you're running. See **open** (a file) for more details.

clustering Linking several computers to one printer (or to any other expensive **peripheral** that isn't constantly used). Also called **shared-resource.**

CMOS (see-moss) An advanced kind of **MOS** technology (the name stands for "complementary metal oxide-silicon"). CMOS chips require less power and generate less heat than the earlier **PMOS** and **NMOS** chips.

CMU Carnegie-Mellon University in Pittsburgh. CMU is an important center of computer research, particularly in the area of artificial intelligence. Also see **computer science.**

COBOL (coe-bawl) A **high-level programming language** which features "English-like" statements and is widely used in business applications. The name stands for "*co*mmon *b*usiness-*o*riented *l*anguage."

code The actual statements or instructions in a program; what programmers produce. *Have you seen his code? What a mess!* See **flowchart** for a sample of some code. For what's meant by "code" in ordinary language, see **encrypt.**

code key What the **control key** is called on some systems.

cokebottle {hacker jargon} Any very unusual symbol that's part of a **character set**—one that looks like a Coke bottle, for example.

cold boot The act of turning a computer on and loading an **operating system** into it. Compare **warm boot.**

column A horizontal position on a line where a character can be put. Thus an 80-column screen is capable of displaying eighty characters on a line.

.COM (dot-kahm) A common **file type** for programs (that is, files that are meant to be executed, as opposed to **data files**). .COM is short for "command."

Sometimes **.BIN** (for "binary") is also used. Compare **.DOC.**

COMDEX (kahm-dex) The "*com*munications and *d*ata processing *ex*position"—a big computer trade show held twice a year, in the spring and in the fall.

command The generic name for anything you tell any **program** to do. As opposed to a **message,** which is anything the computer tells you. See the diagram and explanation at **programming language.**

comment Words added to the actual **code** in a program, so that the programmer can tell what's supposed to be happening at that point without having to go back and figure out the whole program. Comments are ignored by the computer when the program is run.

In **BASIC,** comments are indicated by the abbreviation **REM** (for "remark"). See the illustration at **flowchart** for examples of comments.

compatible Able to work together. *Even though these are both supposed to be standard RS-232 connectors, they're not compatible.*

compiler (kum-PIE-ler) A program that translates the statements of a **high-level programming language** into a lower-level language—often into **machine language.**

All high-level languages have either a compiler or an **interpreter.** Unlike interpreters, which execute each line of the program individually each time the program is run, compilers translate the whole program at once, before it's run. From that point on, you can run the compiled program whenever you want, without having to use the compiler to translate it again.

Compiling is more time-consuming when you're editing a program for mistakes (because you have to recompile the whole program each time you want to check out the effect of a change you've made), but less time-consuming when you want to use a finished program over and over again.

See the diagram and explanation at **programming language.**

component A part of a computer system. The term includes both devices that are part of the computer proper (like **memory boards**) and **peripherals** that connect with the computer (like **printers**, **plotters**, and **OCR readers**).

computer A general-purpose machine for processing large quantities of information. What makes it general-purpose is its ability to be programmed to do different tasks. For a 500-word summary of how computers work, see the special section at the beginning of the book.

early computer research

computer box See **box**.

computer letters Personalized **form letters** produced by a **merge-print program**.

computer-on-a-chip Another name for a **microprocessor**.

computer science What the study of computers is called at universities.
  The big three among computer-science grad schools are often considered to be Stanford, MIT and Carnegie-Mellon. Other schools with strong departments are the University of California at Berkeley, the University of Waterloo (in Canada), the University of Illinois, UCLA, Cornell, the University of Washington, the University of Texas, the University of Wisconsin, USC, Purdue and the University of Rochester.

concatenate (kahn-CAT-uh-nate) A $5 word for a nickel concept—to concatenate files simply means to combine them.

conditional carriage return See **soft carriage return**.

conditional hyphen See **soft hyphen**.

conditional page In word processing, a command that tells the computer to stop during printout and count how many lines there are to the bottom of the page. If there are fewer than the number specified in the command, the printout jumps to the next page. If there are more, it continues on the present page.

This command is used to make sure that a portion of text—a chart or table, for example—appears all on one page, and isn't broken between the bottom of one page and the top of the next. (You just count how many lines there are in the table and put that number in a conditional page command at the start of the table.)

configuration A particular grouping or arrangement of components. *This configuration is specifically designed for graphic artists.*

connect time In **time sharing,** how long you're on the line connected with the computer.

connector conspiracy {hacker jargon} The tendency of some manufacturers (motivated by porcine greed) to make their new products incompatible with older products, by equipping them with new kinds of connectors (physical **interfaces**) that won't fit together with already-existing connectors. Their dumb little hope is that you'll be forced to buy everything new from them; outsmart them and don't buy from them at all.

console A device used to give information to a computer and to get information back from it. It consists of a keyboard and either a CRT or a printer.

"Console" is almost synonymous with **terminal,** with three minor differences:

—the console can be integral to the computer itself, but a terminal must be separate;

—the console is always the main input/output device, but there can be many terminals; and

—there may be certain commands you can enter from the console but not from any other terminal.

contactless key switches See **Hall-effect key switches.**

continuous form paper Paper that comes in a roll, or a series of sheets connected by perforations (which is called **fanfold paper**).

control character What's produced when you hold down the

control key and then strike another key (or keys). Control characters often *do* things—move the cursor, for example—rather than appear in the text themselves (although they sometimes appear on the screen as special symbols).

control key A special key on computer keyboards that—like the shift key—changes the meaning of other keys if it's held down when they're struck. Also see **control character.**

controllable cursor Another name for an **addressable cursor.**

controller A **board** that goes in the computer and controls a **peripheral.**

conversational Another name for **interactive.**

copy A duplicate of a file or a disk, usually in the form of electromagnetic impulses rather than marks on paper (unless it's a **hard copy**).

CP/M One of the most common operating systems for microcomputers, developed by Gary Kildall and published by his company, Digital Research. The original version is sometimes called **CP/M-80,** to distinguish it from later versions like **CP/M-86** and **CP/M-68000.** The name stands for "control program for microprocessors."

CP/M-86 A version of CP/M that runs on machines built around the 8086 or 8088 CPU chip, like the IBM Personal Computer.

CP/M-68000 A version of CP/M that runs on machines built around the 68000 CPU chip.

cps "Characters per second"—a measure of the speed of printers. To convert from cps to words per minute, multiply by ten if you want actual words per minute, and by twelve if you want official, five-character words per minute (see **word** for more on the distinction).

CPU The "central processing unit"—the central part of the computer, the circuitry that actually performs the arithmetic.

In a microcomputer, the CPU is usually all on one **board** (called the **CPU board,** of course) or even on part of a board. The CPU board contains the **CPU chip**—the **microprocessor** which is the actual computing part of the computer. (The CPU chip is sometimes also referred to simply as the **CPU.**)

Also see the special section on how computers work at the beginning of the book.

CPU-bound Another way of saying **processor-bound.**

cr Abbreviation for **carriage return.**

crlf (KUR-lif) {hacker jargon} Abbreviation for **carriage return/line feed.**

crash Noun and verb which mean your computer (or a program you're running on it) has suddenly stopped working—or, worse, is suddenly working wrong (spitting out garbage, giving you false results, etc.). Also see **head crash.**

Cray A line of **supercomputers.** The Cray 1 can perform eighty *million* operations per *second.* Unfortunately, these incredibly powerful machines are used for things like weapons research.

cretinous {hacker jargon} Worthless, stupid, idiotic. See **bogus** for a list of synonyms.

crock {hacker jargon} A program, part of a program, or programming technique that's clumsy, fragile and/or prone to fail. Also—more generally—anything that isn't well designed.

CRT A "cathode ray tube"—a screen like the one on a television set. CRTs are the most common devices used as computer displays.

crufty {hacker jargon} Poorly built, with the connotation that pieces are physically falling off of it (or so it seems).
    Also—disgusting, especially to the touch. See **bogus** for a list of synonyms.

(to) crunch See **number-crunching.**

cursor The marker which tells you where you are on the screen. It usually takes the form of a solid block of light the size of one character, but it can also be a small up-pointing triangle below the line, or an underline. (Some computers and **terminals** let you choose the type of cursor you use.) Cursors sometimes flash or blink, thereby causing eye fatigue and psychosis.
    "Cursor" is a Latin word meaning "runner."

```
<<< APPLE II STOCK QUOTE >>>
          SAMPLE
STATUS AS OF 03/12/79    11:07 EASTERN

       QUOTE WHICH STOCK?     ITT

            BID/CLOSE:    28
            ASK/OPEN:     27 7/8
            HIGH:         27 7/8
            LOW:          27 7/8
            LAST:         27 7/8
            VOL(100'S):      95

            ANOTHER QUOTE? ■
```

the cursor is the square block near the bottom of the screen
COURTESY OF APPLE COMPUTERS, INC.

cursor arrow A key with an arrow printed on it that moves the cursor in the direction indicated.

cursor diamond Four **cursor arrows** or other keys arranged in a diamond, so that the top key moves the cursor up, the right-hand key moves it right, and so on.

cuspy {hacker jargon} Good. Usually applied to programs. The name comes from an acronym of **DEC**'s which stands for "commonly used system program."

customized form letters Personalized form letters produced by a **merge-print program.**

custom software Software you pay a programmer to write specifically for you, tailored to your individual needs. As opposed to **canned software.**

cut & paste If you don't have a word processor, this means cutting up a draft of something you're writing and putting the pieces back together in a different order (usually with tape rather than paste, actually). If you *do* have a word processor, it's a synonym for **block moves.**

cut sheet feeder A device that fits on top of a printer and feeds separate sheets of paper into it. Also see **tractor feed** and **continuous form paper.**

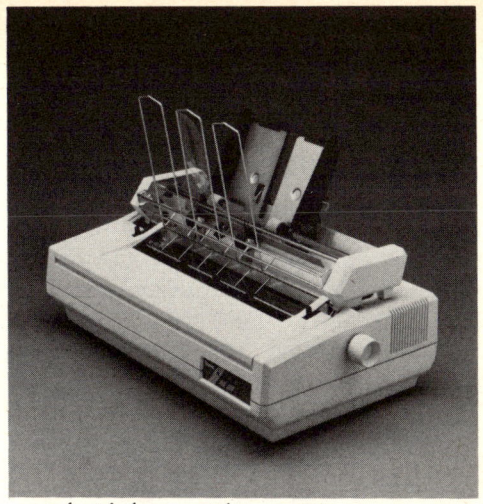

a cut sheet feeder mounted on a printer
COURTESY OF QUME CORPORATION—A SUBSIDIARY OF ITT

CVT A "constant voltage transformer"—a device used to correct high, low or fluctuating line voltage (electricity from your wall sockets) that can wreak havoc on a computer.

Cyber (SIGH-ber) A line of **supercomputers** made by Control Data Corporation.

D

daemon (DAY-mun; sometimes DEE-mun) On **minicomputers** and **mainframes**, a program you don't call up directly, but which lies in wait until certain conditions occur. Sometimes called a **demon**.

You (the user) don't necessarily know that the daemon will be invoked by those conditions, although—on the other hand—you might do something simply because you know it will invoke the daemon. For example, you might send a file to the printer **queue,** knowing that will invoke the printer daemon (which wakes up the printer and tells it to print the file). Compare **dragon.**

daisy wheel A flat, circular device, made of plastic or metal, with characters mounted on it. Certain **formed-character printers** (called **daisy wheel printers**) use it as their **print element.** As the daisy wheel spins at very high speed, a small hammer darts out and knocks specific characters against the ribbon.

a daisy wheel COURTESY OF DIABLO SYSTEMS, INC., A XEROX COMPANY.

data Information—in the widest possible sense. "Data" is the generic name for anything you input to a computer, or anything the computer outputs to you—except for garbage (which is called "garbage"). Also see **GIGO.**

In Latin, "data" is plural, the singular being "datum"—a single fact (literally, it means "a given"). This has been carried over into English, so some people say "These data are interesting." This Latinate usage will soon be obsolete (if it isn't already), replaced by the singular "This data is interesting."

data base Any relatively large accumulation of information that a computer sorts through to find various items. For example, the names, addresses and account information for all of your company's clients would be a data base if they were on a computer. So would the lyrics to all of Bessie Smith's songs. Data bases are made up of **records**.

There are two basic kinds of data bases—private and public. A **private data base** can be the property of an individual or a corporation, and it can be shared with employees, colleagues and friends; but if people are charged for the right to access it, it's considered a **public data base.** There are thousands of public data bases, covering just about every subject area, and several directories that list them.

data base management system Just what it sounds like—a program for handling the information in a data base.

data bus The part of a **bus** that carries data between the various components and **peripherals.** Distinguished from the **address bus,** which is used to locate the data.

data file A **file** composed of data—as opposed to a program, which is a file composed of instructions. A data file might be a letter to your uncle in Tanzania, the addresses and phone numbers of your fellow garlic fanciers, or the point spreads on all this week's NFL games.

data processing Sorting data, performing arithmetic on it, selecting various pieces of it, etc.—as distinguished from **word processing** and other, more specific tasks.

Today "data processing" usually refers to large-scale business computing done on **minicomputers** or **mainframes.** More commonly referred to as **DP** or **EDP** (the "E" stands for "electronic").

data set Another name for a **modem.**

day mode {hacker jargon} Getting up in the morning and going to bed at night. *I just can't hack day mode. The only way I can work 9 to 5 is by starting at 9 p.m. and knocking off at 5 a.m.*

Day mode is supposed to be more virtuous than **night mode** (staying up all night and sleeping most of the day— the mode favored by many hackers). Somehow the people who naturally wake up at dawn all bright-eyed and bushy-tailed (and who consequently begin to punctuate their conversation with snores after eight in the evening) have managed to brainwash most people into believing that their "lark" metabolism is normal and healthy. This metabolic chauvinism is profoundly oppressive to those of us with an "owl" metabolism (which—it's well known—usually correlates with admirable qualities like creativity, intelligence, and loose morals).

As someone who typically goes to sleep around 7 a.m., I've amused myself by imagining a movie poster that reads: "Now, at last, their tragic tale can be told! Helpless victims of deranged metabolisms that wrench them brutally out of bed in the *morning,* these pitiful wretches are condemned to spend their waking hours assaulted by loud noises, shuffling about in huge crowds, squinting into the sun. Yes, horrible as it may seem ... *They Live by Day!*"

DBMS Abbreviation for **data base management system.**

deadlock Like Alphonse and Gaston (who can't get through the door because they keep saying, "After you, Gaston," "No, no, after *you,* Alphonse," "No, Gaston, I insist—after *you*"), a deadlock is a situation where two (or more) processes are stalled because each is waiting for the other to do something first.

One example is when a printer is waiting for the computer to send it more data to print out, and the computer is waiting for the printer to tell it that it's ready to receive more data.

In Europe, a deadlock is usually called a **deadly embrace.** Also see **catatonic** and **wedged.**

GAR SMITH

debugging Getting the mistakes and design errors out of a piece of software or hardware. Also see **Murphy's Law**.

DEC (deck) The usual way of referring to Digital Equipment Corporation.

decimal tab A tab stop that automatically lines up vertical columns of numbers so that their decimal points are all directly above and below each other. Here's an example:

```
288.101
  5.12
   .94611
 19.41
```

dedicated Reserved for one particular use or purpose.

dedicated key A **function key** with only one function; the command it executes doesn't change, and is usually written on it. Cursor arrows are one example; the ESC key is another.

dedicated word processor A computer designed specifically to do word processing, usually with little or no ability to be used as a general-purpose computer.

default What happens if you don't specify something else. *In many word processing programs, single-spacing is the default.*
  The phrase **default value** is sometimes also used. *The default value for the top margin is six lines.*

delimiter A character that's used to separate other characters. The software you use defines what symbols will be considered delimiters, and in what contexts. Some symbols commonly used are commas, spaces, quotation marks, **carriage returns, line feeds** and **form feeds**.
  For example, commas are used as delimiters in MicroPro's MailMerge program. Thus a MailMerge name-and-address listing looks something like this: Mr.,Jack,Twiller,1938 Drain Court,Scranton,PA,18518.

demented {hacker jargon} Said of a program that works as planned but is very poorly designed. *With demented software like this, who needs bugs?* See **bogus** for a list of synonyms.

demon See **daemon**.

descenders The little tails on g's, y's, j's, p's and q's that descend below the line. On some primitive dot-matrix printers and CRTs, they don't actually extend below the line (that is, they lack **true descenders**).

device Any part of a computer (or of anything else) that does one specific job. Thus disk drives are devices, because they do one specific job (permanent storage of data), but a whole computer isn't a device, because it does all sorts of different jobs.

diagnostics A series of **routines** used to diagnose a malfunction.

dial-up port A **port** you can call over phone lines to connect up your **terminal** with a computer. When you use one of the private long-distance phone services like Sprint, MCI or Telesaver, the local access number you call is a dial-up port to their computer (and your terminal is a telephone).

dictionary In a **spelling checker program,** the list of words the program checks text against. A **dictionary program** is another name for a **spelling checker.**

diddle {hacker jargon} To play around with. *Let's diddle with it a little and see if we can't get it to work.*

difference engine See Charles **Babbage.**

digital Broken down into little pieces, which are then treated as numbers. As opposed to **analog.**

A regular clock is an analog device, because its hands move smoothly around the clock face. The hands don't break time up; they just move through it. A digital clock, on the other hand, divides time into many discrete pieces (usually vibrations of a quartz crystal), and then works with those.

Some early computers were analog (the slide rule is one example). But today virtually all are digital, because "digitizing" data (making it digital) has a couple of important advantages. One is that electronic circuits handle numbers much more quickly than physical (analog) devices. Present-day computers divide time into millionths of a second, and data into pieces as small as you want.

Another advantage of digital computers is that there's no slop: numbers don't change, wear down, expand when they get hot, contract when they get cold, and so on.

DIP (pronounced as one word, not as three letters) A "dual in-line package"—what most chips are packaged in. The DIP protects the chip and—with its two rows of pins—connects it to the **board**. See **motherboard** and **chip**.

DIP switch Some DIPs have little switches on them that change how the chip inside functions. For example, on the **video board** in my computer there's a DIP switch that gives me reverse video (dark on light) if I push it one way, regular video (light on dark) if I push it the other.

Because DIP switches are quite small, they're often hard to manipulate, and thus can make you feel like yelling, "Wait till I get my hands on you, you little DIP switch!"

direct-connect modem A **modem** that plugs right into the phone jack (or is directly connected to the phone line in some other way). As opposed to an **acoustic coupler**.

directory A list of files on a disk. (In some **operating systems**, a directory is called a **catalog**, but only in the sense of *all* the files on a disk). In **CP/M, PC DOS** and some other operating systems, the command **DIR** displays the directory.

dirty power Electricity coming into a computer that has any one of several things wrong with it—**noise, spikes,** consistently low voltage, etc. Corrected by **CVTs, line filters, surge suppressors,** etc.

disk (sometimes spelled **disc** for some ungodly reason) The generic name for **floppy disks** and **hard disks**.

disk controller See **floppy disk controller**.

disk drive A device that writes information onto—and reads information off of—a floppy disk or a hard disk. Disk drives are the most common **storage devices** on microcomputers.

As the drive spins the disk at high speed, an arm (something like the tone arm on a record turntable) moves back and forth to various concentric **tracks** on the disk, and absorbs—or deposits—information (by means of the read/write **head** that's mounted on it).

diskette The bland, official name for a **floppy disk**.

display What a computer uses to show you what it's doing. Usually a display is a CRT, but there are also **gas-plasma displays, flat-panel displays,** etc. Also called a **monitor,** or simply a **screen**.

a combination floppy/hard disk drive with the cover off (the floppy is on the left and the hard disk is on the right) COURTESY OF MORROW DESIGNS

distributed processing In a multiuser system, taking the load off the main **CPU** by assigning some of the computational duties to each terminal or to a number of different CPUs.

distribution disk Another name for a **master disk**.

DMA "Direct memory access"—a common form of **memory-mapped video**.
 Also—a kind of disk **controller** that allows transfer of data to and from the disk at very high speeds.

DOA "Dead on arrival." Used to describe a product that doesn't work when you take it out of the box.

.DOC (dot-DAHK) A common **file type** for **text files**. It's short for "document." **.TXT** (for "text") is also used. Compare **.COM**.

document A generic name for anything you write (particularly if you write it on a computer).

documentation Written information about computer hardware and software—instructions, training manuals, on-screen tutorials, **comments** in programs, reference materials of all sorts.

DO-loop (DOO-loop) A section of a program that's repeated until a certain condition is met.

(to) **do protocol** {hacker jargon} To interact with someone or something in a clearly defined manner. The **Jargon File** gives the example of "doing protocol with the check." This includes asking the waiter or waitress for it, deciding if it's going to be split unevenly or evenly between everybody, figuring out how much everybody owes, adding on the tip, collecting the money, making sure everybody gets the right amount of change, and paying the bill.

DOS (dahss or dawss) "Disk operating system." See **operating system**. Also abbreviated **OS**.

Some manufacturers also use DOS, without further qualification, to refer to their own operating system. Thus Apple calls simply DOS what the rest of us know as Apple DOS, and IBM refers to PC DOS as just DOS.

dot What a period is (almost always) called in the world of computers. Also see the listing under . at the end of the book.

dot command In many word processing programs, a kind of **embedded** command that's distinguished from the actual text by being placed on a line beginning with a period. Some programs let you put more than one dot command on the same line.

Here are a few examples of dot commands in the word processing program I use:

```
.bfon ulon hyon
.rm73 lm13 tm2 bm3
```

The first line tells the program to turn the boldfacing, underlining and automatic hyphenation features on. The second line tells it to put the right margin at 73 and the left margin at 13, and to leave a top margin of two lines and bottom margin of three.

dot matrix (MAY-trix) A system for forming letters and other characters out of small dots. All CRTs and many printers use dot matrixes.

The more dots in the matrix, the higher the quality of the character formed in it (i.e., the higher the **resolution**). Typical low-resolution dot matrixes are five dots by seven (a total of 35 dots available to build each character out of) or seven by nine (63 dots); high-resolution dot matrixes range up to eleven by thirteen (143 dots) and beyond.

The old-fashioned (i.e., Latin) plural is **matrices** (MAY-tri-seez); the more informal plural is **matrixes**.

dot-matrix printer Any of several kinds of printers that produce characters (and other images) by creating them out of dots in a matrix. The two basic kinds of dot-matrix printer are **impact** (which push the needles that make up the matrix against an inked ribbon and then into the paper) and **non-impact** (which use electricity or heat to bring the image up out of the paper without touching it). Compare **formed-character printer**.

double-density A system for putting information onto a floppy disk that crams twice as much into the same space as **single-density**.

double-sided Refers to floppy disks that store information on both sides, rather than just on one.

doublestriking See **overstriking**.

down Not working (as opposed to **up**).

download To transfer data to a nearby computer from a distant computer. Compare **upload**.

downtime The length of time a system is **down**. Often talked about as a percentage of total time. *Our downtime on this damned machine has been averaging 20%.*

DP Abbreviation for **data processing**.

draft mode On **multipass printers,** draft mode is used for fast printouts, which are done without **overstriking**. The text produced doesn't look great, but it's good enough to use for editing a draft.

dragon On **minicomputers** and **mainframes,** a program which can't be called up by the user but is used by the system to perform some sort of secondary or internal job. One example would be a program that keeps track of everybody who's working on the system at a given moment. Most **fortune-cookie programs** are also dragons.

Unlike a **daemon,** a dragon operates more or less all the time.

drive A short name for a **disk drive**.

-driven A suffix that means "structured around." Thus "menu-driven" refers to programs that use lots of **menus** and "example-driven" refers to manuals chock-full of examples.

driver A piece of software or hardware that **interfaces** a particular device to the rest of the system. *That new printer driver of yours is really hot.*

drop-ins Characters not typed by you that appear in your data, because the system is malxfunctxioningx.

dropouts Characters that are deleted from your data because the system is malfunctioning. Drpouts look lik ths. Usualy ther arn't so mny. If u cn rd ths, u cn gt a gd jb. . . .

DTRT {hacker jargon} An abbreviation for "do the right thing"—sometimes used to implore the computer to read your mind. Compare **DWIM**.

dumb Having little or no computational ability of its own. Said of terminals, keyboards, printers, etc. Compare **smart** and **intelligent**.

(to) dump Either to transfer all the information from one part of a system to another (*Dump this file to disk so we can clear memory*) or to throw it away completely (*OK, let's dump this garbage and begin again*).

duplex Capable of transmitting data in both directions—that is, to *and* from a given location. As opposed to **simplex**. Also see **full duplex** and **half duplex**.

Dvorak keyboard A particular arrangement of keys that strives to make typing easy—unlike the standard **QWERTY**, which was designed to make typing hard.

This key arrangement was devised in 1932 by Dr. August Dvorak of the University of Washington, after he had spent many years studying the movements of typists' fingers and the frequency of letter combinations in English words. Unfortunately, it's little used. Also see **keyboard**.

DWIM {hacker jargon} An abbreviation for "do what I mean"—used to tell a computer to read your mind. Compare **DTRT**.

dynamic RAM Memory which the computer must refresh (i.e., **rewrite**) at frequent intervals (500 times a second is common). It's cheaper than its opposite, **static RAM,** but it's also more susceptible to **glitches** and other kinds of **dirty power.**

E

E A symbol meaning "to the ___ power," often used when you can't display superscripts (it stands for "exponent"). So, for example, 10E6 is equal to 10^6 (one million).

(to) edit In word processing, to create and/or alter text. Some examples of editing functions are inserting, deleting, moving blocks of text around, and searching for particular words and phrases and replacing them with others. Compare **format.**

editor The part of a word processing program that edits the text (as opposed to the **formatter**). Sometimes an editor is a stand-alone program (in which case it's often called a **text editor**).

EDP Abbreviation for "electronic data processing." Also see **data processing.**

EIA The Electronic Industries Association, a trade organization. Also see **RS-232.**

eight-bit chip A **CPU chip** that processes data eight bits at a time—as opposed to faster, more expensive chips that handle data in sixteen-, 32-, or 64-bit chunks. The 8080, Z80, 6502 and 6800 are a few examples of eight-bit chips.

8/16-bit chip A **CPU chip** that handles data in sixteen-bit chunks internally but takes it in and sends it out eight bits at a time. The 6809 and 8088 are two examples.

8080 An **eight-bit chip** made by Intel. The 8080 was the first to be widely used in personal computers.

8085 An **eight-bit chip,** an upgrade of the 8080. Made by Intel.

8086 A **sixteen-bit chip** in the 8080 family. Made by Intel.

8088 An **8/16-bit chip** made by Intel that's used in the IBM Personal Computer and other machines.

electric pig In England, one of the names for a garbage disposal unit in a sink. So called because it performs one of the functions of a pig (it eats the garbage).

Electric pigs have nothing to do with computers, of course, but it's one of my favorite names and I've always wanted to put it in a dictionary.

GAR SMITH

electronic bulletin board A computer (or part of one) that maintains a list of messages so that people can call up (with their computers) and either post a message or read the ones that are already there. Electronic bulletin boards are often specific; some of the **information networks** have scores of different ones.

electronic cut & paste Another name for **block moves.**

electronic mail The sending and receiving of typed messages between users on a computer network or on a multiuser system.

electronic spreadsheet program Software that (in effect) creates a large work sheet on which you can do financial projections, budgeting and planning. VisiCalc was the first of these, and its many imitators are sometimes called Visi-Clones.

electrosensitive printer A printer that uses electricity to form characters on specially treated (usually aluminum-coated) paper.

elegant Said of programs, this means they are written in a clean, efficient manner, without a lot of sloppy patchwork, **hacks** and **kluges. Tasteful** is a synonym. Also see **flavorful.**

elite type A size of type which fits twelve characters into each horizontal inch. Compare **pica type.**

(to) embed (em-BED) In word processing, to insert a command into your text (the most common methods are putting it on a line beginning with a period or placing backslashes around it). When the word processing program gets to an **embedded command,** rather than printing it out, it obeys it.

Compare **print-time commands.** See **dot command** for some examples. **Imbed** is an alternate spelling.

EMI "Electromagnetic interference"—another name for **noise.**

emulation One machine or **operating system** acting like another—accepting the same commands and behaving in the same way (except that an emulation almost always runs slower than the original). *The Apple III can emulate the Apple II and thus run most of the software written for the Apple II.*

encrypt (en-KRIPT) To jumble or otherwise disguise the contents of a program (or other file) so that unauthorized people can't copy it or use it. The word "code" is not used in this context, since what a program is made up of is called **code** whether it's encrypted or not.

end users People who use computer products themselves (as opposed to **OEM**s, who resell them).

ENIAC (EN-ee-ak) The first electronic digital computer, built by John Mauchly, J. Presper Eckert, Jr., and others at the University of Pennsylvania's Moore School; it was completed in 1943. The name stands for "electronic numerical integrator and calculator." Eckert and Mauchly went on to build **UNIVAC**.

ENIAC COURTESY OF APPLE COMPUTERS, INC.

J. Presper Eckert with ENIAC COURTESY OF INTERNATIONAL BUSINESS MACHINES CORPORATION

ENTER A special key on some keyboards that begins execution of a command. On most systems, the RETURN key fills this function. (Often the ENTER key is just a relabeled RETURN key, but some keyboards have both keys.)

EOF "End of file." Mostly used to refer to the symbol that marks the end of a file.

EOL or **EOLN** "End of line."

EOM "End of message."

EOT "End of transmission."

epsilon {hacker jargon} A small quantity of anything. *The cost is epsilon but the risk is significant.*

EPROM (EE-prahm) An "erasable programmable read-only memory" chip—a kind of **PROM** that's particularly easy to reprogram.

ergonomics Another name for **human engineering**.

error message A piece of text that appears on the screen to tell you something is wrong.

The helpfulness of error messages varies tremendously. Some are masterpieces of clarity: LOAD THE DISK, STUPID. Others are as inscrutable as 13th-century Lithuanian: ERROR P12R—MACRO PARAMETER OVERFLOW EXCEEDS LOCAL ENVIRONMENT.

ESC or **ESCAPE** A special key found on computer keyboards. Its function depends on the software you're running, but as its name implies—it's commonly used to interrupt a command that's executing, or to move you from one part of a program to another.

excl (EX-kul) {hacker jargon} A spoken abbreviation for "exclamation mark." **Bang** and **wow** are also used.

execution time How long it takes a command—or series of commands—to execute.

expandable Said of a computer that can be improved and made capable of performing new functions, usually by putting extra **boards** into it.

expansion interface Some computers which don't have **expansion slots** nevertheless support an expansion interface. It allows you to add disk drives, more memory, and other enhancements. It's also called an **expansion board** or **expansion card**.

expansion slots Extra slots in the **motherboard** which are empty when the computer comes to you and are used for adding new boards that expand what the computer can do.

extension Another name for a **file type**.

F

facsimile A picture, chart, map, etc. transmitted over some distance. Abbreviated **FAX**.

fan-fold paper Continuous form paper made up of single sheets with perforations between them. It folds into the box like a fan or an accordion.

fatal bug A programming or design error that crashes a program, forcing you to **reboot** and lose all your work since the last time you saved. People who release software before making sure that all the fatal bugs are out of it should be locked in a room with a Moonie for six months.

GAR SMITH

fatal error A mistake you make that crashes the program. If you think it's the program's fault, you call it a **fatal bug**. Actually, any well-designed program should make fatal errors impossible. So—in my view—*all* fatal errors are the result of fatal bugs.

FAX (pronounced as one word) Abbreviation for **facsimile**.

FDC Abbreviation for **floppy disk controller**.

feature Something good a piece of software or hardware does.
There's a saying in the computer business that the easiest way to deal with a **bug** is to document it (mention it in the manual) and call it a feature. Of course you can't do that if the bug does something really horrible, but there are many "features" you'll run across that could only have begun their careers as bugs. Also see **misfeature**.

BUG   FEATURE   GAR SMITH

feedback Information on how a process is proceeding, delivered to whatever controls the process. For example, you might have a device that senses how much heat is generated by a chemical reaction and feeds this information back to the computer that controls the reaction. If things get too hot, the computer slows the reaction down; if they get too cold, it speeds the reaction up.

feep {hacker jargon} Another name for the beep that **terminals** make at various times to get your attention—to tell you that you've reached the end of a line, for example. The softer the sound is, the more likely it is to be called a feep rather than a beep.

field A specific portion of a **record.** For example, if the record is in a mailing list program, there will be—at least—a name field, an address field, a city field, a state field and a field for the zip code.

In the field means anywhere but the factory where a computer—or any piece of hardware—is manufactured. *We've designed this system so that just about any repair can be made in the field.*

field-upgradable Said of hardware, this means that it's capable of being enhanced **in the field** (at the store where you bought it, for example), rather than having to be sent back to the factory.

FIFO (FIE-foe) A **queue** in which the *f*irst item *i*n is the *f*irst one *o*ut. Compare **LIFO.**

file A bunch of data, or a program. What makes it a file is simply that you call all of it by one name.

file name The label you use to identify a file, so that the computer knows what you're talking about when you want to load it into memory, store it onto disk, etc.

file type In **CP/M, FLEX, PC DOS** and some other **operating systems,** a three-letter addition to a file name. It follows a period at the end of the name, and indicates—naturally—the type of file it is. A few common file types are .DOC ("document"), .BAK ("backup") and .COM ("command"—i.e., a program, rather than a data file). Also called an **extension** or simply a **type.**

find and replace See **global find and replace.**

firmware Software stored in a **ROM,** rather than on a disk. The advantage is that you don't have to load it into **RAM** to make it work; the disadvantage is that it's much harder to change.

first generation Computers that used vacuum tubes for their switches—like ENIAC and UNIVAC. (Some people refer to these as second-generation computers, and call the first generation those computers—like IBM's Mark I—that used mechanical relays.) See the chart at **fourth generation.**

fixed disk A **hard disk** that can't be removed from its drive. A **Winchester** is one example.

fixed point The normal way of representing numbers, without the use of exponents. Called fixed point because the decimal point (or binary point or whatever) stays in the same place and the number of digits to the left of it varies. See **floating point** for a fuller explanation.

flag A marker.
Also—to mark.

(to) flame {hacker jargon} To rant.
Also used as a noun. For an example of a flame, see **day mode**.
To **flame on** is to rant and rant and rant.

flat panel Any one of several technologies that substitute for **CRTs** and allow for much flatter, less bulky shapes. There are two main types: **phosphorescent** and **nonemitter**.

flavor {hacker jargon} Variety, type, kind. *Formatting commands come in two flavors: embedded and print-time.*

flavorful {hacker jargon} Beautiful; aesthetically pleasing. When talking about a program, **tasteful** and **elegant** are synonyms. See **bogus** for a list of antonyms.

Flex An **operating system** for 6800/6809 machines.

flexible disk A bland, corporate name for a **floppy disk**.

flexible diskette Ditto.

floating point A way of representing numbers so that there's always just one digit to the left of the decimal point (or binary point or whatever), and the actual size of the numbers is indicated by exponents. So, for example, 1941 in the common, everyday **fixed-point** notation becomes 1.941 E3 (1.941×10^3) in floating-point notation.

Floating-point notation is widely used in scientific work (and, in fact, **scientific notation** is a synonym for it). Certain computers are designed specifically for doing large numbers of floating-point operations.

To understand how floating point gets its name, consider three (fixed-point) numbers: 13742.6, 23 and .00146. In floating point, they become 1.37426 E4, 2.3 E1, and 1.46 E−3. The decimal point floats over to the same position in each number; only the exponent (10 to some power) shows where it came from.

In fixed point, you know how large the numbers are by

where their decimal points are fixed; E0 (that is, an exponent of 10^0, which is equal to 1) is assumed for all numbers.

floppy or **floppy disk** A device for the permanent storage of computer data. The information is stored magnetically on material similar to recording tape. It's called a floppy to distinguish it from rigid, **hard disks**—which hold more data and get to it more quickly, but cost more money.

Floppies are round and come in square protective envelopes made of cardboard that are about a sixteenth of an inch thick. There are two basic sizes—those that are eight inches in diameter, and $5\frac{1}{4}''$ **minifloppies**. (New **microfloppies**—smaller than four inches in diameter—have also been introduced.)

two common sizes of floppy disks—$5\frac{1}{4}''$ minifloppy and 8'' floppy

floppy disk drives   COURTESY OF MORROW DESIGNS

Floppies come **hard-sectored** and **soft-sectored, single-sided** and **double-sided, single-density** and **double-density**. A typical single-density, single-sided, soft-sectored 8" floppy holds about 240**K**.

floppy disk controller The **chip** or **board** that controls a floppy disk drive.

flowchart A graphic representation of how a program, or system, works (or is supposed to work). Standard symbols are used to indicate things like branching questions. In programming, flowcharts are an intermediate step between an **algorithm** and actual programming **code**.

Say, for example, you wanted to write a program to count the number of words in a piece of text. The algorithm for that might read something like this:

1. Specify the text to be checked. (In this case, we'll assume it's already in memory, that it starts at **address** 2000H, and that a 0 indicates the end of it.)

2. Define "word" as any group of characters separated by either spaces or carriage returns.

3. Start a counter at 1. Each time a space or carriage return is reached, add 1 to the counter. When the end of text is reached, the counter will equal the number of words.

A flowchart based on this algorithm is shown on the next page, followed by the actual **code** that will do the job (in the **high-level language** called **SPL/M**). The words on the right, with /"'s at the beginning and at the end, are **comments** which remind the programmer what the code on the left does.

(to) flush To empty a portion of memory of its contents. *I could barely contain my excitement when she suggested we flush the buffer.*

In hacker jargon, "flush" also means to go home after a day's work. *Six o'clock—time to flush.*

font A typeface and size. The most common sizes for fonts produced by computer printers are pica (ten characters to the inch) and elite (twelve characters to the inch). Computer fonts come serif or sans serif, regular or bold, italic or Roman, expanded or condensed, and so on.

foo {hacker jargon} A name often given to a temporary file (one that will only exist for a short time).

foo? {hacker jargon} When conversing on computer termi-

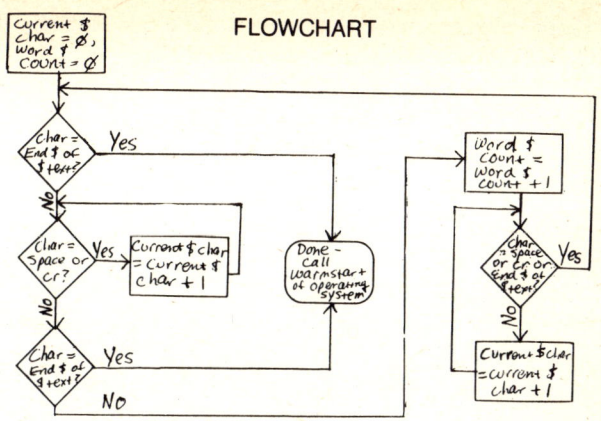

FLOWCHART

CODE

```
1000H:;                          /*locate program at this address*/
2000H:DCL TEXT(4000) BYTE;       /*4000-byte array of text at this 2000H address*/
DCL WORDSCOUNT ADDR,             /*number of words found*/
    CURRENTSCHAR ADDR;           /*current character in text being looked at*/
DCL ENDSOFTEXT LIT '0',          /*a '0' marks end of the text in memory*/
    SPC LIT '20H',               /*ASCII value of a space*/
    CR LIT '0DH';                /*ASCII value of a carriage return*/

CURRENTSCHAR=0;                  /*initialize to look at first text character*/
WORDSCOUNT=0;                    /*initialize - no words yet found*/

DO WHILE TEXT(CURRENTSCHAR) <> ENDSOFTEXT;        /*look at all chars to end*/
   DO WHILE (TEXT(CURRENTSCHAR) = SPC) OR
            (TEXT(CURRENTSCHAR) = CR);     /*words separated by spaces, cr's*/
      CURRENTSCHAR=CURRENTSCHAR+1;    /*ignore a run of spaces and/or cr's*/
   END;
   IF TEXT(CURRENTSCHAR) = ENDSOFTEXT THEN BREAK; /*end:break from do-while*/
   WORDSCOUNT=WORDSCOUNT+1;          /*else have found 1 more word: count it*/
   DO WHILE (TEXT(CURRENTSCHAR) <> SPC) AND
            (TEXT(CURRENTSCHAR) <> CR) AND
            (TEXT(CURRENTSCHAR) <> ENDSOFTEXT);
      CURRENTSCHAR=CURRENTSCHAR+1;   /*ignore rest of letters in word*/
   END;
END;

CALL WARMS;                      /*return to operating system warmstart*/
EOF                              /*end of program*/
```

nals, a greeting that means "Are you there?" "What's happening?" or "Am I intruding?", depending on the context.

footer In word processing, a piece of text (usually a single line) repeated at the bottom of each page. The text can vary (as, for example, in footers containing page numbers). The footer on this page is: 61. Compare **header.**

(to) format To prepare text for printout. Formatting involves setting the page length, margins, line spacing, character spacing, page numbering, headers, footers, line justification and the like. Compare **edit.**

To **format a disk** is to prepare it to accept information.

formatter The part of a word processing program that formats the text (as opposed to the **editor**). Sometimes a formatter is a stand-alone program (in which case it's sometimes called a **text processor**).

formed-character printer The most common kind of **letter-quality printer,** it produces images the same way typewriters do—by pushing something in the shape of a character against an inked ribbon and into the paper. Formed-character printers are relatively slow and relatively expensive. Compare **dot-matrix printer.**

Most formed-character printers use a flat, circular device called a **daisy wheel** on which the characters are mounted. NEC Spinwriters use a **thimble.** The daisy wheel or thimble spins very fast and a high-speed hammer hits it when the desired character is right in front of it.

form feed The command and/or symbol that moves the printout on to the next page. The name comes from the fact that the "form" (paper) "feeds" (moves up) to the start of the next sheet. Sometimes called a **carriage-control character.** Compare **line feed.**

form letter program Another name for a **merge-print program.**

FOR ... NEXT A programming statement in many **high-level languages** that tells the program to keep doing something a given number of times. Also called **FOR ... TO.**

Forth A **high-level programming language** whose many fans are a reminder that "fan" is short for "fanatic." Forth produces very compact **code** and programs written in it can actually be shorter than some versions of the same program written in **assembly language.** (Because it's so close to assembly language, Forth is sometimes called a **low-level**—rather than a high-level—language. But there's also an advantage to this; it gives you a good feeling for how the machine thinks.) Forth uses the awkward **Polish notation,** in which 2 + 3 is written 2, 3 +.

The language was developed in the late '60s by Charles Moore when he was working at a home-furnishings company in Amsterdam, New York (just a few short miles from the middle of nowhere). The first thing Forth was used for was designing carpet patterns, but its fame began with its use as a controller for telescopes, first at Kitt Peak Observatory in Arizona and then at many other places.

The story behind the name is this: Moore felt that he was creating a fourth-generation programming language, and thus wanted to call it Fourth. But the computer he was using only accepted five-letter file names, so he dropped the "u."

FORTRAN An early **high-level programming language,** designed by IBM, that is still widely used in scientific applications. The name stands for *"formula translation."*

fortune-cookie program On multiuser systems, a program that randomly sends graffiti to your screen to keep you amused while you're waiting for programs to run. Any sort of graffiti can be used, whether related to computers (*Your password is embarrassingly obvious*) or not (*Be liberated—make him sleep on the wet spot*).

A fortune-cookie program is usually a **dragon,** but it can also be a **daemon** (if, for example, it's called up when you **log out**—to give you one parting shot).

fourth generation Computers based on **integrated circuits** (in the system that calls computers based on mechanical relays the first generation). Most people call computers based on integrated circuits the third generation. See the chart below.

Computer generations

Usual reckoning	Switch technology used:	Alternate reckoning
(no name)	electromechanical	first generation
first generation	vacuum tubes	second generation
second generation	transistors	third generation
third generation	integrated circuits	fourth generation

4004 The first popular **CPU chip,** introduced by Intel in November 1971.

Franz LISP A version of the **LISP** programming language developed at the University of California's Berkeley campus by Richard Fateman et al. It can accept and run programs written in other kinds of LISP without modification.

Fredkin Prize A $100,000 prize, administered by Carnegie-Mellon University, which will go to the programmer of the first computer that wins the world chess championship. In the meantime, the interest on the $100,000 is used to sponsor (and provide prize money for) computer chess tournaments.

By mid-1983, just about any chess master could beat even the best chess-playing computer (Belle, from Bell Labs)—although a computer program called Cray Blitz had managed to win the Mississippi state chess championship against human opponents.

frequency The number of times something repeats in a given period of time. Usually applied to cycles per second of an electrical current. Also see **hertz**.

friction feed Moving paper through a printer by means of rollers pressing against the platen, the way a typewriter does. Compare **tractor feed** and **pin feed**.

fried {hacker jargon} Not working because of hardware failure. *I'm afraid your memory board is completely fried.*

Also said of people who are exhausted or burned out. *After debugging this crock for 36 hours, I'm completely fried.*

See **bogus** for a list of synonyms.

friendly See **user-friendly**.

(to) frobnicate (or frob) {hacker jargon} To aimlessly manipulate a knob or other control. *Stop frobbing the contrast on that CRT and come play space war with me.*

Twiddle and **tweak** have similar meanings, but (to quote the **Jargon File**) "'frob' connotes aimless manipulation; 'twiddle' connotes gross manipulation (often a coarse search for a proper setting); 'tweak' connotes fine-tuning."

Let's say you're turning a knob on a television set. If you're carefully adjusting it, you're tweaking it. If you're turning it more or less randomly but looking at the screen to see what effect you're having, you're twiddling it. If you're just turning the knob because turning the knob is fun, you're frobbing it.

frobnitz (or frob) {hacker jargon} Like "widget," a generic name for any small object. *Their new printer has this little frobnitz on the side that lets you flush the buffer.* Since the term "frobnicate" is also shortened to "frob," it's possible to speak of *frobbing a frob*—aimlessly manipulating a dial or other small object.

The plural—in imitation of Yiddish—is **frobnitzim**. Compare **glork**.

full duplex Able to transmit two messages in opposite directions, independently of each other. Normal telephone lines are full duplex. Compare **half duplex** and **simplex**.

full-screen editing Being able to move the cursor all over the screen to alter text (the only way to go, by the way). Compare **line editor**.

function key A special key that doesn't produce a character on the screen, but rather executes a command or series of commands. There are two basic kinds: **programmable function keys** (or **soft keys**), whose function varies with the software you're using, and fixed-function **dedicated keys**.

G

ga {hacker jargon} An abbreviation for "go ahead"—widely used in typed conversations on computer terminals when two people begin typing at the same moment ("ga" tells the other person to go first).

gas plasma A kind of **flat-panel** display, widely used when the display is only one line high.

gate A generic name for the kind of electronic switches that make up the **CPU, memory,** and other thinking parts of a computer. Each gate is made up of about ten to twenty transistors.

germanium A chemical element (atomic number 32) sometimes used instead of silicon in the manufacture of **chips**.

getting (a file) Another name for **loading** (a file).

giga- (GIG-uh) A prefix indicating one billion—or, sometimes, 1,073,741,824 (that is, 2^{30}). Abbreviated **G**.

gigabyte A billion **bytes** (or 1024 **megabytes**; 1,073,741,824 bytes). Compare **megabyte** and **kilobyte**.

gigahertz A frequency of a billion times a second; usually applied to cycles of an electrical current. Abbreviated **GHz**. Compare **hertz, kilohertz** and **megahertz**.

GIGO (GUY-go) "Garbage in, garbage out." In other words, you can't expect a computer to outsmart your stupid mistakes. (In imitation of **FIFO** and **LIFO**.)

glare Reflections from the surface of a screen, caused by lights, windows, etc.

glitch A sudden voltage surge or burst of electromagnetic **noise** that causes a piece of hardware to malfunction.

Also used more broadly to mean any suddenly occurring problem or interruption. From the Yiddish *glitshen,* to slip. Also see **snivitz**.

glob What the * symbol is called on some systems. The more common name is **star**. **Splat** is also heard, but "asterisk" almost never. Also see the listing under * at the end of the book.

global editor In word processing, the part of an **editor** that makes changes everywhere in a document, not just where the cursor is.

global find and replace In word processing, the ability to find a **string** (i.e., a word, phrase or whatever) anywhere it appears in a document, and to substitute another string for it. Also called **global search and substitution.**

glork {hacker jargon} A generic name for just about anything. Unlike **frobnitz,** it isn't restricted to physical objects.

"Glork" is also used as a reflexive verb, meaning to do harm to oneself. *My program just glorked itself.*

GOK {hacker jargon} "God only knows"—used to save keystrokes when conversing on a terminal.

GOSUB (pronounced as syllables, not letters) A programming statement in BASIC that tells the program to execute a **subroutine** and then return to the statement which follows the GOSUB statement

In other **high-level languages,** the same effect is produced by a CALL statement, or simply by inserting the name of the subroutine. Compare **GO TO.**

GO TO (or **GOTO**) (pronounced as words, not letters) A programming statement in **high-level languages** that tells the program to jump to another statement out of the normal sequence and continue from that point on.

Because they make programs difficult to follow and understand, GO TO statements are forbidden in some languages (and discouraged in virtually all). Also called a **jump.** Compare **GOSUB.**

GPIB The "general-purpose interface bus"—another name for the **IEEE-488.**

gritch {hacker jargon} A complaint. Also used as a verb and sometimes doubled to **gritch gritch,** which is more or less equivalent to "bitch, bitch, bitch—that's all you ever do."

(to) **gronk out** {hacker jargon} To cease functioning. *This bletcherous keyboard just gronked out again!*

When said of people, it means to go home and/or to sleep. *Well, I see the sun has struck the sultan's turret with a shaft of light—time to gronk out.*

You can also talk about people being **gronked**—i.e., very tired or sick.

(to) **grovel over** {hacker jargon} To work interminably and without apparent progress. Both people and computers can grovel over things. If you're *really* groveling over something, you're **groveling obscenely.**

H

H An abbreviation which indicates that the number preceding it is **hexadecimal**.

hacker A computer enthusiast; someone who enjoys programming and fools around with computers. Also (and consequently), a computer expert.

To hack is to work on something (*This week I'm hacking the terminal driver*), often with the implication of habitually (*I hack LISP*) and/or idly (Hacker X: *What are you doing?* Hacker Y: *Oh, nothing much. Just hacking*).

How's hacking? is a common greeting between hackers. **A hack** is the programming equivalent of a quick fix—sort of like a **kluge**.

Many examples of **hacker jargon** are included in this dictionary (see **bogus** and **day mode** for some samples). The ultimate resource for hacker jargon is the famed **Jargon File**.

hacker   GAR SMITH

hair {hacker jargon} The complexity and complications that make something difficult. *Each of them is simple enough on its* *own, but interfacing them involves infinite hair.* From the common slang word **hairy**—"risky, challenging."

half duplex Able to transmit messages in opposite directions but not simultaneously. Walkie-talkies are an example of half duplex. Compare **full duplex** and **simplex.**

Hall-effect key switches When you depress a key on one of these, a plunger passes through a magnetic field, and this sends the signal from the keyboard to the computer. Since the key and the switch never touch, these are also called "contactless" key switches. Hall-effect key switches are a relatively new technology, and most keyboards don't have them.

handshaking When transmitting data, a system for letting each of the computers or **peripherals** involved know when to talk and when to listen.

hanging indent Another name for an **outdent.**

hard When part of a computer term, "hard" has the general meaning of permanent, unchanging (except in the case of **hard disk,** where it literally means rigid, firm). Compare **soft.**

hard carriage return A command to always break a line at a given point, regardless of whether or not it's full. Equivalent to a **line feed.** See **soft carriage return** for more details.

hard copy Actual paper with text on it, as opposed to what you see on your screen or copy onto a disk. Hard copies are usually **printouts.**

hard disk The next step up from a **floppy disk.** Hard disks hold more data and get to it more quickly, but cost more money. Hard disks consist of a magnetically sensitive coating applied to a ceramic or aluminum disk which spins at a very high speed. Also see **fixed disk** and **Winchester.**

Because most hard disks are sealed in their drives, they can't be exchanged the way **floppies** can. For this reason, **backups** are usually done onto floppies or magnetic tape.

A hard disk's **read/write head** "flies" closer to the disk than the width of a particle of cigarette smoke. Since one such particle inside the drive could cause a **head crash,** smoking is usually banned in rooms where hard disk drives operate.

a hard disk drive disassembled COURTESY OF MORROW DESIGNS

hard hyphen A hyphen that always prints out, as opposed to a **soft hyphen,** which only prints out if it falls at the end of a line.

hard-sectored Describes a kind of **floppy disk** that doesn't let the **operating system** choose where to record information on it, because it's been divided into unalterable **sectors**—usually by means of a ring of small holes that run around the disk. As opposed to **soft-sectored.**

hard space Another name for a **no-break space.**

hardware The actual physical components of a computer system; the machinery. Distinguished from **software.**

hardwarily {hacker jargon} In hardware, or with respect to hardware. *We decided to implement this feature hardwarily.* As opposed to **softwarily.**

hard-wired Built right into the hardware. **Hard-wiring**—using hardware rather than software to program something—saves the (trivial) bother of loading a program, but makes changing the program infinitely more difficult.

hash Visual static on the screen.

head A short name for the **read/write head**—the part of a disk drive that actually puts the information on, and pulls the information off of, the disk. Other magnetic storage devices (like tape drives—or, for that matter, tape recorders) also have heads. Heads "fly" extremely close to the disk—at distances like 100 microns (1/30th the thickness of a human hair).

head crash In disk drives, the actual touching of the disk by the read/write head. At the bare minimum, this erases some of the data on the disk; at the grisly maximum, it destroys the whole disk drive.

header In word processing, a piece of text (usually a single line) repeated at the top of each page. The text can vary (as, for example, in headers containing page numbers). The header on this page is: Arthur Naiman. Compare **footer**.

hertz The number of cycles of an electrical current (or of anything else) per second; a measure of **frequency.** For example, one hertz means once per second. Abbreviated **Hz**. Compare **kilohertz, megahertz, gigahertz.**

 Named after the German physicist Heinrich Hertz (1857–94).

hexadecimal A system of representing numbers in base sixteen. The numerals 0 through 9 mean what they normally do and then A = ten, B = eleven and so on up to F = fifteen. Thus 16 in decimal notation is represented in hexadecimal by 10 (one sixteen and no ones), 44 is 2C (two sixteens and a twelve), and 255 is FF (fifteen sixteens and a fifteen).

 Hexadecimal notation is used because it converts into **binary numbers**—which is what computers think in—more readily than decimal numbers do, and yet it's much more compact and easy to deal with than binary notation.

 Often abbreviated **hex.** Hexadecimal numbers are also indicated by putting the letter **H** at the end of them (or **0x** at the beginning of them). *The ASCII code for ESCAPE is 1BH.*

high- (or **higher-**) **level languages** Programming languages which are fairly close to natural languages like English, with commands that each translate into several instructions to the computer. As opposed to **assembly languages,** which talk directly to the computer.

Unlike assembly languages, high-level languages usually work on many different types of machines (just so long as a **compiler** or **interpreter** has been written to interface the language with the **CPU chip** the machine is based on). High-level languages are easier to program in than assembly languages, but generally produce programs that are less efficient and run slower. **Pascal, LISP, FORTRAN** and **COBOL** are examples of high-level languages.

Certain languages, like **BASIC** and **Forth,** are sometimes called **low-level languages,** because they don't have certain features of—or are somewhat closer to assembly language than—other high-level languages.

See the diagram and explanation at **programming language.**

(to) **highlight** To make parts of the text brighter than the rest of the text on a screen, or to show them in reverse video, in order to distinguish them from the rest of the text.

high-persistence phosphor Unlike the less-expensive kind of **phosphor** that coats the inside of television screens, high-persistence phosphor holds an image much longer. It's widely used on computer monitors. See **interlace** for a discussion of one way around having to use high-persistence phosphor.

Hollerith card The standard **punched card** used for storing data, with eighty columns and twelve rows. Invented by the American statistician Herman Hollerith (1860–1929), who proposed using them to help sort data for the 1890 census.

COURTESY OF INTERNATIONAL BUSINESS MACHINE CORPORATION

The reason many **CRTs** have 80 columns is simply that Hollerith cards do. Hollerith cards aren't used much any more, except in antiquated data-processing departments.

hologram A three-dimensional image produced in thin air by lasers interacting with each other—the computer display of the future.

home The upper left corner of the screen. (This is where the computer's heart is.)

home computer Not a very precise term—it simply means any relatively small microcomputer used at home.

home row The row of keys on the keyboard where touch typists rest their fingers between keystrokes. On a **QWERTY** keyboard, the home row is asdfghjkl . . .

hook {hacker jargon} An extra piece of software or hardware included to make later additions easier. *The program won't support proportional spacing in this release, but the hooks for it are in, so it won't be hard to add it later on.*

horizontal scrolling Moving text on the screen to the left, so the right end of lines too long to fit on the screen can be seen. (Naturally this puts the beginnings of the lines off the screen to the left, until you scroll back the other way.)

HPIB The "Hewlett-Packard interface bus," from which the industry-standard **IEEE-488** bus was derived.

human engineering Designing a product as if human beings were going to use it (that is, making a product easier and more comfortable for human beings to use). Also called **ergonomics.**

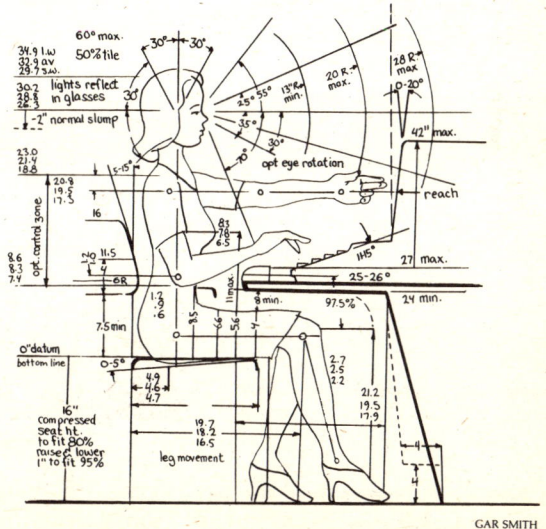

GAR SMITH

hungus (HUNG-iss) {hacker jargon} Unmanageably huge. *This is one hungus piece of code.* (Probably from the common slang expression "humungous.")

Hz Abbreviation for **hertz**.

I

IBM DOS Another name for **PC DOS**.

IBM 360 series A line of **mainframe** computers which dominated large-scale computing applications in the late '60s.

IBM 3740 format A format for storing information on **floppy disks** that has become the standard for 8" floppies. (Unfortunately, there is no standard format for **minifloppies**.)

IC Abbreviation for **integrated circuit**. Also called a **chip**.

IEEE-488 (eye triple-ee) An **industry-standard parallel interface**. IEEE stands for Institute of Electrical and Electronic Engineers.

IF ... THEN A programming statement in **high-level languages** that tells the program to perform certain computations if certain conditions prevail—for example, in a tax-preparation program, if the taxable income exceeds (say) $10,000. Compare **GO TO**.

imbed Alternate spelling for **embed**.

impact printer Any printer that forms characters by hitting the paper. There are many different kinds, including most **dot-matrix** and all **formed-character** printers. Compare **nonimpact printer**.

(to) implement To make something work. *We hope to have PIE Writer implemented on that machine the end of next month.*

incremental spacing A synonym for **microspacing.**

indexer A program that generates an index (and sometimes also a table of contents) for a document.

industry-standard Theoretically, this describes a piece of hardware or software that's the same no matter who makes it or what machine you use it on. In practice, however, many manufacturers only *say* they follow industry standards (see **connector conspiracy**). For example, there are many nonstandard interfaces advertised as **RS-232.** As Schiller put it, "Against stupidity the gods themselves contend in vain." Ditto for greed.

(to) initialize To clear memory (or a disk or some other area) of previous information, so that it's ready to be used again.
   Also—to set the variables in a program to their initial **values.**

infinite {hacker jargon} Extreme, or a lot of (but not actually an infinite number of). **Infinite hair** means extreme difficulty.

information network A large computer **time-sharing** facility that gives you access to a number of **public data bases** and provides services like **electronic mail, electronic bulletin boards,** discount shopping and the like. CompuServe and The Source are two examples.

ink-jet printer An advanced technology in which letters are formed by electrostatically aiming and forming a jet of ink as it shoots toward the paper.

(to) input To introduce data into a computer.
   Also—the data introduced. *With input like this, no wonder your output is bogus.* Also see **GIGO.**

insert mode When a word processing program is in this mode, it inserts text at the **cursor,** pushing all text that follows right and down. Opposite of **writeover mode.**

(to) install Many **applications programs** come to you with an **installation program** on the same disk. You go through the installation program once and tell it what kind of equipment you have, so that it knows how to put information on the screen in a readable manner, make the printer work right and so on. This is called "installing the program."

The installation program modifies the applications program in accordance with what you've told it, so from that point on you don't have to bother with installation anymore (unless you want to change something, in which case you just run through the installation program again).

instant print A feature of some word processing programs, this lets you use the system as a typewriter. With instant print, each time you hit a key, the character is immediately transmitted to the printer. (This is different from the normal state of affairs, where characters are stored in memory, then **formatted** and sent to the printer all together.)

instruction One single operation you tell the computer to do. **Commands** within programs and **statements** in programming languages both translate into series of **machine language** instructions. See the diagram and explanation at **programming language.**

instruction set All the basic instructions a **CPU chip** understands. Different kinds of chips have different instruction sets (although some, like the 8086 and 8088, share a common one).

integrated circuit An electronic circuit that has been shrunk down and put on a chip. More commonly called an **IC**. Also called a **chip.**

intelligent Even smarter than **smart.**

interactive Involving a dialog between you and the computer, so that each command you give elicits a more or less immediate response. As opposed to **batch processing.** Also called **conversational.** Also see **real-time.**

interface The hardware and/or software needed to connect components, computers, or any combination thereof. Also see **user interface.**

To **interface** is to design, set up or program such a connection. **To interface with someone** is used by corporate androids as a synonym for "to relate to" or "to cooperate with."

interlace A system for putting images on a **CRT** that reduces flicker. Half the lines in the picture—every other line—are transmitted first, then the other half is sent; together they make up one complete image. This sounds as if it would *increase* flicker but it actually helps, because it doubles the number of pictures sent to the screen each second (even though each picture is missing half its lines).

Interlace is common on television sets, but isn't much used on computer monitors, because their **high-persistence phosphor** eliminates the need for it.

internal storage Another name for **memory**. Also called **internal memory.**

interpreter A program that executes the statements of a **high-level programming language** directly, rather than translating them into **object code** the way a compiler does.

All high-level languages must have either an interpreter or a compiler. See **compiler** for more on the difference between them. Also see the diagram and explanation at **programming language.**

interrupt A signal sent by a program or a component (like the keyboard or the printer) asking the computer to stop what it's doing to do something else. When the requested task is completed, the computer goes back to what it was doing before. Some systems don't allow interrupts, but others allow multiple ones (which then have to be prioritized).

Most **multiuser** and **multitasking** systems are **interrupt-driven,** which means they handle multiple jobs by having the **operating system** interrupt the computer many times each second.

(to) invoke To call up (a program, or part of a program). *The MARKFIX program is automatically invoked once you've finished reviewing the spelling errors.*

I/O "Input and/or output" (of information).

I/O board A **board** that controls the input and output of information between the computer and devices like disk drives. Also sometimes called an **I/O processor.**

I/O-bound Refers to processes that are slowed down by the amount of time it takes to input and output the information involved—that is, the CPU has to sit around and twiddle its thumbs waiting for I/O to happen.

Distinguished from **processor-bound.** (Also distinguished from Alabamy-bound.)

I/O port A place where other devices can connect with a computer to input and/or output data.

I/O processor A separate **microprocessor** chip or board used just to handle I/O, thereby taking this time-consuming task off the main **CPU**'s hands. Also see **I/O board**.

IPL "Initial program load"—on some IBM systems, a synonym for **booting** the system.

ips "Inches per second"—a measure of a tape's speed.

ISIS (EYE-sis) An **operating system** for **8080**-based systems. The name stands for "Intel system implementation supervisor"—although here, as with BASIC, it's likely that the acronym came before (not after) the full name.

ISO The International Standards Organization, which—like **ANSI**—maintains records of thousands of voluntary standards in a number of different fields.

J

jack The place where something is plugged in. The jacks on a computer where you plug in cables from peripherals are called **ports**.

Jacquard loom An automatic loom, the first to weave in patterns, invented around 1800 by the Frenchman Joseph-Marie Jacquard (1752–1834). It was the first programmable machine of any kind. Large, stiff punched cards told it what pattern to weave.

Jargon File A short, informal dictionary of computer terms and **hacker jargon** that's reachable on the **ARPAnet**. It was

the Jacquard loom COURTESY OF INTERNATIONAL BUSINESS MACHINE CORPORATION

compiled by Guy L. Steele, Jr., Raphael Finkel, Donald Woods and Mark Crispin, with assistance from the MIT and Stanford AI communities and Worcester Polytechnic Institute, and with additional contributions from other people at various places—particularly Geoff Goodfellow and Richard Stallman. Much of the hacker jargon in this book was obtained from the Jargon File (although the accuracy or inaccuracy of my definitions is, of course, solely my responsibility).

For a long time, only excerpts from the Jargon File had been published; if you wanted to read it in its entirety, you had to know someone with access to the ARPAnet (who would then look for a file named "GLS; JARGON" at MIT-AI or MIT-MC, or "AIWORD.RF[UP,DOC]" at SAIL, and print it out). But now Guy Steele tells me that the whole Jargon File will be published in the fall of 1983. If you enjoy the taste of hacker jargon I provide in this book, you might want to check out the more extensive treatment of the subject in that one.

jock {hacker jargon} A programmer whose programs tend to achieve their results by means of brute force rather than elegance.

joystick A little ... well ... stick that can be pointed in any direction to move the cursor (or any other symbol) around the screen. Joysticks are much used in video games. The name comes from the similar device that controls airplanes.

J. Random See **random.**

jump In programming, an instruction to execute some instruction other than the next one in the program. Also called a **GO TO** statement.

justification Making lines of text straight at the margin.

Left justification (a straight left margin) is the most common format for typed text, and **justification to both margins** is the most common format for typeset text. The term **right justification** is almost always used as a synonym for justification to both margins, but technically it refers to a format where the *right* margin is straight and the *left* is **ragged** (which isn't very useful).

The phrase "justified text" without further explanation implies justification to both margins. This text is set justified to both margins.

K

K Abbreviation for **kilo-,** which means a thousand—or, sometimes, 1024 (that is, 2^{10}).

Usually K is short for **KB**—a **kilobyte** (1024 bytes). Sometimes, however, it's short for **kilobit**—1024 *bits.* (In this dictionary, I always use K to refer to a kilo*byte.*)

Kansas City Standard An early standard (now obsolete) for placing information on cassette tapes. It only works at the very slow speed of 300 characters a second. **KCS** is the abbreviation.

Katakana (kah-tuh-KAH-nuh) One of the three Japanese alphabets (and the only phonetic one), Katakana is mostly used to transcribe non-Japanese terms. (You run across the term when reading about terminals and printers that can produce the Katakana character set.)

Here are the words "computer jargon" in Katakana:

コンピューター ジャーゴン

KB or **Kbyte** (KAY-bite) Abbreviations for **kilobyte**—1024 bytes.

keyboard Oh, you know what a keyboard is. The important thing to mention is that it can be bought either separately or as part of a **terminal.** Keyboards vary in terms of how they feel to type on, how **smart** they are, the number of keys they contain, the layout of the keys, etc.

The standard layout is called **QWERTY,** which was intentionally designed to be clumsy. (The first typewriter was so inefficient that its keys jammed when they were arranged in any sensible way. So the inventors rearranged them to slow typists down.) Other, more sensible arrangements have been introduced (see **Dvorak**).

the PCD-Maltron Keyboard COURTESY OF PCD MALTRON LTD.

At least one manufacturer (in England) has changed the shape of the keyboard in order to better fit the actual shape of the hands, the typical distance between them, and the varying strengths of the fingers. The keyboard they make is called the **PCD-Maltron,** and it looks like it was designed by Claes Oldenburg or Salvador Dali.

key bounce A problem with some keyboards whose **key switches** are poorly designed. You hit the key once but it registers twice (or more).

keypad A mini-keyboard, made up of special-purpose keys. A **numeric keypad**—the ten number keys arranged in a rectangle—is the most common example. Numeric keypads are usually part of a keyboard, but they (and other kinds of keypads) can also be bought separately.

key switch When you push down on a key, you close a switch. When the key switch is closed, the character on the key you pushed is transmitted to the computer (and usually also displayed on the screen).

key tops The part of the keys your fingers hit.

Also—little labels supplied with a piece of software that are designed to be stuck to the top or front of the keys to remind you of where various commands are.

keyword A significant word (or phrase) in the title (or text) of a document which can be used to identify and/or retrieve the document. So, for example, if you wanted to find references to South Africa in a large **data base** of magazine articles, you might search for any of the following keywords: "South Africa," "apartheid," "gold," "diamonds," "U.S. investment" and "slavery."

KHz Abbreviation for **kilohertz.**

(to) kill To delete (a file, for example, or a word).

Also—to abort (a process).

kilo- (KILL-uh, not KILL-oh) A prefix indicating one thousand—or, sometimes, 1024 (that is, 2^{10}). Abbreviated **K.**

kilobaud A thousand bits per second. Used to measure the speed at which data is transmitted.

kilobit 1024 bits. Sometimes abbreviated **K** (but usually K stands for "kilo*byte*"—which is equal to eight kilobits).

kilobyte (KILL-uh-bite) 1024 bytes. Equal to about 170 actual words or 205 official, five-letter, typing-test words. A kilobyte fills about two-thirds of a double-spaced page (with 1" margins and pica type). Both the amount of memory in a computer and the capacity of a floppy disk are usually measured in kilobytes. Abbreviated **Kbyte, KB** or just **K**.

kilohertz A frequency of a thousand times a second; usually applied to cycles of an electrical current. Abbreviated **KHz**. Compare **hertz, megahertz** and **gigahertz**.

(to) kluge (klooj) {hacker jargon} To solve a problem by patching, rather than finding the root cause and correcting that. *I didn't have time to fix it right so I just kluged it.*

Also—the result of such patching. *This whole program is one big kluge.* Also called a **hack**. The adjective is **klugy** (KLOOJ-ee). From the German *klug*, clever.

kluge   GAR SMITH

KSR "Keyboard send/receive." Refers to printers that have their own keyboards and thus can give instructions to a computer, as well as merely print what the computer tells them to. Compare **R/O**.

L

language See **programming language**.

large-scale integration See **LSI**.

laser printer An advanced technology in which characters are formed by a laser and made visible by electrostatically attracting dry ink powder, as in a photocopying machine.

LCD "Liquid crystal display"—a common sort of **flat-panel** display. LCDs are common on calculators and digital watches. (They're the ones that you can see in sunlight, but that you have to shine a light on to see in the dark. Usually they're colored black.) On an LCD computer monitor, LCDs replace the **pixels** of a CRT. Compare **LED**.

learning curve A curve which graphs how performance improves as learning progresses. Typically used in a loose, general way: *You're a little farther along the learning curve than I am.*

A learning curve is usually steep at the beginning, because there's a tremendous amount of initial and background information you have to absorb when learning about a new subject. Then the curve tends to level off, as more and more of what you encounter is stuff you already know.

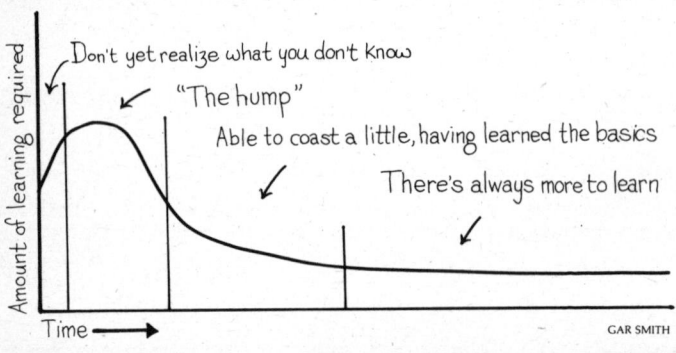

a typical learning curve

Sometimes people talk about being **over the hump** of the learning curve, by which they mean they've gotten past the basics to the more gentle part of the slope.

learning programs Programs that teach you things rather than take your data and process it. Distinguished from **applications programs, systems software** and games. See the diagram and explanation at **programming language**.

LED "Light-emitting diode"—a common type of **flat-panel** display. LEDs used to be quite common on calculators and digital watches, but have now mostly been replaced by **LCDs**. (LEDs are the ones that shine in the dark, but wash out in the sunlight. Often they're colored red.) When LEDs are used in computers, it's usually for single-line displays.

left justification Printing out text so that the left margin is straight and the right is **ragged**—the most common format for typed text. See **justification** for the other alternatives.

legal {hacker jargon} Allowed; meeting all the requirements set forth by a particular program or system. *OLDJUNK.CRP is a legal file name in CP/M.*

letter-quality printer A printer that produces printouts you wouldn't be ashamed to send out as business letters. **Formed-character printers** are the main kind, but **multi-pass printers** are also capable of producing letter-quality text. (Precisely where to draw the line between letter-quality and **near-letter-quality** is, of course, a matter of opinion.)

Life A sophisticated and elegant computer game, invented by John Horton Conway, which simulates the growth of single-celled organisms (although not necessarily any that actually exist on earth).

LIFO (LIE-foe) A **queue** in which the *l*ast item *i*n is the *f*irst one *o*ut. Compare **FIFO**.

light pen A device you use to point to things, or to draw designs, on a special CRT screen which has been sensitized to respond to it.

line conditioner A device which combines a **surge suppressor**, a **line filter** and a **CVT**. Also called a **line stabilizer**.

line editor A type of **editor** that requires you to specify the line (and word) you want to make your changes on, rather than letting you simply move the **cursor** there.

Line editors were common before CRTs became the typical **terminal** (since **printer terminals** don't even have cursors); now they're pretty much obsolete. If you have a screen, what you want is a **screen editor**.

line feed In word processing, a command and/or symbol that moves the cursor (or printout) to the next line of text, whether or not the present line is full. Line feeds are usually generated by the **RETURN** key.

For example, as I type this on my computer, I hit the RETURN key at the end of every paragraph, and an extra time between each entry (to give me a blank line there). My word processing program inserts little left-facing arrows (which are the symbols it uses to indicate a line feed) on the screen at each of those points. When it comes across one of these arrows during printout, it moves down to the next line.

Usually the line feed character also tells the computer to execute a **carriage return,** which moves the printout (or, when you're editing, the **cursor**) to the first space of the line. This combination is called, naturally enough, a **carriage return/line feed.** Compare **form feed.**

line filter A device to correct electromagnetic interference (more commonly known as **noise**) that comes in over the power line. Also called a **line isolator.**

line printer This is not a very precise term. Strictly it means a printer that prints a whole line at a time—in other words, very rapidly—but it's sometimes used to describe any **dot-matrix** printer. For example, Radio Shack's Line Printer VII only prints 30 **cps**—hardly a line at a time.

line stabilizer Another name for a **line conditioner.**

linker A program that links other programs, or parts of programs.

LISP (pronounced as one word) A **high-level programming language** designed primarily to run on large systems and widely used in **artificial intelligence** work.

The name comes from "*list p*rocessing," because LISP is basically oriented toward handling data in the form of lists. One variety is called **Franz LISP.**

listing A **printout** of the actual **code** of a computer program.

load To copy a file from disk (or some other storage medium) to the computer's memory. Opposite of **save.** Sometimes also called **getting** a file.

To **load a disk** means to put it into the disk drive, so that it's engaged.

local network A network of computer equipment confined to a small area—like one office or one building—and connected by **dedicated** wires. A network of computers all in Chicago (say) and connected by phone lines would not be a local network. Sometimes also called a **local area network.**

logged In **CP/M,** refers to the disk drive (and therefore to the disk) that will be accessed if you don't specifically ask for a different one. In many other **operating systems,** called the **default** drive or disk.

logic The actual **CPU** and other related **chips.** *The logic is right here, on this board.* Also see **shared-logic.**

logical {hacker jargon} Having a meaning which doesn't necessarily correspond to reality. Here's an example: San Francisco is basically north of Silicon Valley. So if you get on the freeway going from the latter to the former, you're going "logical north," even though you may be heading due west at the time (because the freeway makes a loop). By the same token, Interstate 80 from New York City to San Francisco is "logical west," even though it heads due north near Davenport, Iowa, due south near Salt Lake City, and south-south-*east* through Berkeley and Richmond, California.

"Logical" can (and usually does) refer to things other than direction. For example, you might refer to a guest host on *The Tonight Show* as "logical Johnny Carson." Also see **virtual.**

logic seeking and logically summing Logic seeking is the ability of some printers to go immediately, without any intermediate stops, to the first point on the page where a character will appear. Logically summing is the ability to jump over several horizontal or vertical spaces in one fell swoop, instead of having to clunk along one line and one space at a time. Both these capabilities speed up printouts significantly.

(to) log in On a multiuser system, to identify yourself to the computer so you can use it. To be **logged in** is to be using the system. Also see **log-in name, log out** and **password.**

log-in name The name by which a multiuser system knows you. You can use your actual name if you want (although, since there's a limit to how long a log-in name can be, you usually can't use your whole name). But the fun is in devising some new name for yourself. It's a little like thinking up a personalized license plate.

In addition to a log-in name, you usually also need to think up a **password.** This gives you even more opportunity to pretend you're a secret agent (or a Shriner).

LOGO (LOW-go) A **high-level programming language** developed at MIT by Seymour Papert and his colleagues, intended primarily for children. Although easy to learn and to use, LOGO is nevertheless quite powerful. Also see **turtle graphics.**

According to Wallace Feurzeig of **BBN,** who thought the name LOGO up, it comes from the Greek word *logos,* which means both "word" and "idea." It's meant to emphasize the connection between informal, linguistic ways of thinking and more formal, mathematical ones—as Papert puts it, to indicate that LOGO is "primarily symbolic and only secondarily quantitative."

(to) log out On a multiuser system, to terminate your connection; to stop using the computer. Also see **log in.**

look-alike A piece of software that imitates another company's software so closely that users of the original program hardly have to learn anything new to use the look-alike, except for the added features the look-alike typically offers (i.e., they can still use all the commands they've already learned to use with the original program). One example is a word processing program called NewWord, which imitates the popular WordStar. Compare **work-alike.**

loop A series of instructions in a program that gets repeated over and over—that is, as soon as the end of the loop is reached, the program immediately starts again at the beginning. This goes on until a certain condition is met—or, in the case of an **endless loop,** forever.

(to) lose {hacker jargon} To fail. *Whenever it reaches this point, the program loses.* The phrase **deserve to lose** is also common. *Anyone who tries that brain-damaged approach deserves to lose.*

Loser can refer to a program or a person. **Real loser** is also widely used. *Of course this software's a real loser; look at the loser who wrote it.* **Losing** is the adjective. Also see **luser**.

Loss refers to something which fails. *What a moby loss that idea was!* The result of a failure, the damage done, is called **lossage** (LAWSS-ij). *This bletcherous bug caused a fair amount of lossage.* Extreme lossage is called **stoppage**. Compare **win, winner,** etc. See **bogus** for a list of synonyms.

Lovelace, (Augusta) Ada, (Countess of) (1815–52) First daughter of the English poet Lord Byron, Ada Lovelace was a mathematical genius who worked with **Charles Babbage** on his **analytical engine** and is generally considered to have been the first computer programmer.

Unfortunately, she was also a victim of the age she lived in. As a woman, only her initials were allowed to appear on work she published. Although she was one of the few people who understood the analytical engine and who could clearly explain how it worked, her identity remained a secret.

Lovelace and Babbage took to betting on horseraces to

COURTESY OF CULVER PICTURES, INC.

finance development of the analytical engine and lost heavily. Ada had to pawn her family jewels to pay her debts. She died of cancer at 36—the same age her father died at. A new programming language, **Ada,** is named after her.

low-level languages A term sometimes applied to languages like **Forth** and **BASIC** which (although technically **high-level languages**) are either closer to **assembly language** or lack certain capabilities of other high-level languages. (Some people feel this distinction is unjustified.)

lpm "Lines per minute"—the least meaningful way to talk about printer speeds, since the number of characters per line can vary. Lpm is a useful term only in the case of *true* **line printers,** which print thousands of characters per second on lines of a standard length.

lpr or **lpt** Abbreviations for **line printer.**

LSI "Large-scale integration"—**integrated-circuit** technology that allows the equivalent of between 1000 and 50,000 transistors to be crammed onto a single chip. See the chart at **chip.**

luser (LOO-zer) {hacker jargon} A derogatory way to refer to a **user.** (Hackers tend to look down on anybody who doesn't share their skills—and their obsessions.)

M

M Abbreviation of **mega-,** which means one million—or, sometimes, 1,048,576 (that is, 2^{20}).

machine Another name for a computer.

machine-independent Capable of running on, or interfacing with, a variety of different computer systems. Said of programs, languages, interfaces, etc.

machine language The actual **binary** instructions a computer understands. All compiled **high-level** and **assembly-language** statements must be translated into machine language before a computer can obey them. See the diagram and explanation at **programming language.**

machine-readable Refers to information in a form that a computer **peripheral** can read. Universal Product Codes—those little black bars on packaged goods that can be read by computerized supermarket cash registers—are one example; documents typed in **OCR** font are another.

macro A command which stands for a series of smaller (micro) commands. As a (simple) example, you might have a word processing macro—.PP, say—that means "start a new paragraph" and is composed of two smaller commands:
   1) leave one line blank; and
   2) indent five spaces.
Whenever the computer comes across the macro .PP in a piece of text, it will execute those two commands.

magic {hacker jargon} Arthur C. Clarke once said that if an alien culture's technology is sufficiently advanced beyond our own, it will seem to us to be magic, without any conceivable rational explanation. Hackers use the word "magic" in a similar sense—to refer to things that are unexplained so far, or too complicated to explain. *The new version has a couple of magic features I think you'll really enjoy.*

magnetic media A generic name for **floppy disks, hard disks,** tapes, magnetic cards, and any other object or substance that stores data in the form of magnetic impulses.

mailbox A special **file** where incoming messages transmitted to you on your computer network (or directly over phone lines) are stored. Also see **electronic mail.**

mailing list program A program that maintains names, addresses and related data and prints out labels of them. Most mailing list programs will also sort **records** into alphabetical order, zip code order, and so on.

mainframe A very large computer (only **supercomputers** are more powerful). Mainframes are larger than **minicomputers** and much larger than **microcomputers.**

Also—another name for a computer **box,** regardless of its size.

main routine See **routine.**

main storage Another name for **memory.** Also called **main memory.**

map A record of where various pieces of information are stored (in memory or on a disk, for example).

Mark I An early computer which used mechanical relays for its switches. Developed at IBM's facilities in Endicott, New York, by Howard Aiken of Harvard and a team of IBM engineers headed by Clair Lake, it was completed in 1944.

The same name was given to a computer built at Manchester University. This English Mark I is generally considered the first to have run an alterable stored program (in 1948).

the IBM Mark I   COURTESY OF INTERNATIONAL BUSINESS MACHINES CORPORATION

mass storage Another name for **storage.**

master disk The actual disk you get from a software store or publisher, with the program you bought on it. Also called a **distribution disk.** Compare **work disk.**

Also, used by software publishers to refer to the disk they make their distribution copies from.

MB Abbreviation for **megabyte**—1024 **kilobytes.**

MBASIC (EM BAY-sic) "MicroSoft BASIC"—the first variety of **BASIC** to run on microcomputers. It was written by Bill Gates, who founded MicroSoft. (The present version of MBASIC has evolved a great deal from the original.)

MDOS (EM doss) Another name for **PC DOS**.

media A shorthand way of referring to **magnetic media**.

medium-scale integration See **MSI**.

meg {hacker slang} A **megabyte.** *It comes with 128K but it's expandable up to a meg.*

mega- A prefix indicating one million—or, sometimes, 1,048,576 (that is, 2^{20}). Abbreviated **M**.

megabyte 1024 **kilobytes;** 1,048,576 **bytes.** Abbreviated **MB**. Compare **kilobyte** and **gigabyte**.

megahertz A frequency of a million times a second; usually applied to cycles of an electrical current. Abbreviated **MHz**. Compare **hertz, kilohertz** and **gigahertz**.

memory The part of a computer that uses **integrated circuits** to retain information electronically. There are two main kinds of memory—**RAM** and **ROM**. RAM is used for the short-term retention of information (i.e., until the computer is turned off). ROM is used to store programs which are seldom or never changed.

    Storage is the long-term retention of information on external **magnetic media** like disks or tapes. The table below summarizes the differences between RAM, ROM and storage devices:

	RAM	ROM	Storage devices
Means of retention	electronic	electronic	magnetic
Speed of access	very fast	very fast	varies, but never as fast as memory
Permanent?	no	yes	yes
Easy to change?	yes	no	yes

A lot of conflicting terminology surrounds the concepts of memory and storage. If RAM were the only kind of memory, I could make a nice simple distinction between the two by saying that memory implies temporary retention of data and storage implies permanent retention. The latter statement is true but not the former; ROM complicates things.

In this book, when I use the term "memory" without qualification, I'm referring to RAM. Whenever possible, I try to steer you away from terms that use the word "storage" to describe nonpermanent memory (**main storage,** for example) or that use the word "memory" to describe permanent storage on magnetic media (**auxiliary memory,** for example).

memory-mapped video A system for transmitting information to a screen by reading it directly from the memory or from the **bus** of the computer. As opposed to **terminal mode.** A **bit-mapped display** is one type of memory-mapped video; **DMA** is another.

menu A list, displayed on the screen, of commands you can choose from.

menu-driven Said of a program which uses menus extensively.

merge-print program A program that lets you produce **personalized form letters** and the like by combining information from various sources (including mailing lists) during the actual printing of each document.

message Text that appears on the screen when the computer wants to tell you something. Compare **command** and **prompt.**

MHz Abbreviation for **megahertz**—a million cycles per second.

micro- A prefix meaning "one millionth."

"Micro-" is also used more loosely, to mean "very small" (as in "microcomputer," "microspacing," etc.).

microcomputer (or **micro**) The smallest of the four sizes of computers, a micro can be carried in your arms (at least the **box** can, and often the whole system). Compare **minicomputer, mainframe** and **supercomputer.**

Home computers and personal computers are both microcomputers. A micro can cost as little as a hundred dollars, but you'll probably have to spend well over a thousand to get the capabilities you want.

microfloppy A **floppy** less than 4" in diameter.

microjustification The ability of some word processing programs, when working with printers that have **microspacing,** to justify lines by adding little slivers of blank space between letters within words, as well as between words. Not to be confused with true **proportional spacing.**

microminiaturization Probably the longest word in the English language actually in daily use (by nonpedants). It means reducing the size of something several orders of magnitude smaller than if you merely miniaturized it. **Integrated circuits (chips)** are one product of microminiaturization.

micron (MY-krahn) A millionth of a meter; about four hundred-thousandths of an inch (.00004″).

microprocessor The actual computing power of a computer, squeezed onto a tiny chip (thirty years ago it filled rooms). Also called an **MPU chip,** or simply an **MPU** (for "microprocessor unit"). The board on which it's mounted is called a **microprocessor** (or **MPU) board.**

A microcomputer's **CPU chip** is always a microprocessor, but microprocessors are also used to do secondary tasks (like **I/O**) on some computers. Only the central, master microprocessor is called the CPU (although you will often hear people refer to a computer's CPU chip simply as "its microprocessor").

microsecond A millionth of a second. Compare **millisecond, nanosecond** and **picosecond.**

microspacing A feature of some printers which allows them to move distances (typically) as small as a 120th of an inch horizontally, or a 60th of an inch vertically. Microspacing is used to do **shadow printing** and **microjustification.** Also called **incremental spacing.**

millisecond A thousandth of a second. Compare **microsecond, nanosecond** and **picosecond.**

minicomputer (or **mini**) A mid-sized computer, larger than a **microcomputer** but smaller than a **mainframe** (and much less powerful than a **supercomputer**). In size, the box is usually comparable to a small refrigerator.

minidiskette Another name for a **minifloppy.**

minifloppy A **floppy** $5\frac{1}{4}″$ in diameter.

MIS Abbreviation for "management information system" (how's that for bland, meaningless corporatese?). An **MIS manager** supervises the choice and use of computers in a large company.

misfeature {hacker jargon} This is sort of intermediate between a **feature** and a **bug**. Misfeatures work OK in most situations but turn out to have a dark side in other situations—usually ones which were unforeseen (or nonexistent) when the product was first introduced. Getting rid of a misfeature often requires overhauling the basic structure of a program. The **Jargon File** gives this example: *Well, yeah, it's kind of a misfeature that file names are limited to six characters, but we're stuck with it for now.*

MIT-AI The artificial intelligence lab at the Massachusetts Institute of Technology in Cambridge, Massachusetts—an important center of computer research. Also see **computer science**.

mnemonic (nuh-MAHN-ik) Aiding memory.

Mnemonics are commands (or anything else) whose names have been made easy to remember, usually because they derive from a word that describes what they do. For example, the command "control-P" to *p*rint out is mnemonic; the command "control-J" to get on-screen help is not.

moby (MOE-bee) {hacker jargon} Big (the word comes from Moby Dick, of course). *And this is the one I call my moby disk drive—it holds thirty megabytes.* Also—complex.

"Moby" is sometimes used by one hacker when addressing another to indicate respect, admiration and/or friendship. *So, moby wizard, how's hacking?*

mode A way of operating (for example, **writeover mode**).

In hacker jargon, "mode" is also applied to people (see **day mode** and **night mode**).

modem (MOE-dum) A device that lets computers talk to one another—or terminals talk to computers—over phone lines. There are two basic kinds—**direct-connect** and **acoustic coupler**. Modems are sometimes called **data sets**.

"Modem" is short for "*mo*dulator-*dem*odulator." A *modulator* takes the digital signals produced by a computer and turns them into audible sounds, so that they can be carried over a phone line. A *demodulator* takes the audible sounds off the phone and converts them into digital signals a computer can understand.

modem board A card that plugs into a computer's motherboard and functions as a **modem** (usually it has a phone-company modular plug attached to it on a cord, which you snake out through a hole in the back of the computer and plug into the wall jack for your phone).

Although modem boards take up less space than modems (and are more convenient for that reason), they're less likely to be portable from one machine to another.

monitor Usually this word simply refers to a **CRT**—the screen on which you see your work. Also called a **display** or simply a **screen**.

But "monitor" also has a technical meaning—a program (or collection of programs) that controls certain basic aspects of a computer's operation.

MOS (sometimes pronounced moss, other times em-oh-ess) "Metal-oxide semiconductor"—a technology used in highly microminiaturized chips like **LSI**s.

motherboard A slotted **card** in the computer **box** that other cards are mounted into. Also called a **card cage** or a **backplane**.

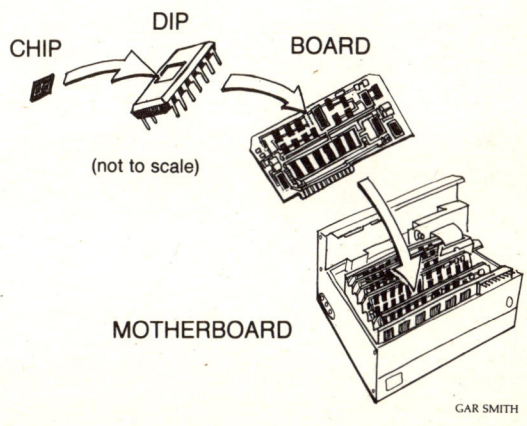

GAR SMITH

mouse A device used for moving the **cursor** on some systems. It's a small box with one to three buttons on the top, attached to the rest of the system by a cord. When you roll the mouse around on any flat surface, a roller ball (or wheels) on its bottom senses the movement and transmits it to the computer over the cord. The computer then moves the cursor on the screen the same distance in the same direction. (The buttons are used for giving commands.)

The mouse is said to be easier and more natural to use than **cursor arrows,** cursor movement commands, etc. On the other hand, it forces you to take your hand off the keyboard.

The patent for the mouse is held by **SRI**. Mice have been around for a while, but only began to get a lot of attention when they were used on the Xerox Star and then on the Apple Lisa. They get their name from the fact that they're small, (usually) gray, have tails (the cord), and scurry around. Compare **CAT** and **rotary control knob**. Also see **Xerox PARC**.

a mouse COURTESY OF APPLE COMPUTERS, INC.

MP/M "Multiprogramming control program for microprocessors"—a multiuser version of **CP/M**.

MPU The "microprocessor unit"—another name for a **microprocessor**. Also called an **MPU chip**. The board on which it's mounted is called an **MPU** (or **microprocessor**) **board**.

ms Abbreviation for **millisecond**.

MS DOS Another name for **PC DOS**.

MSI "Medium-scale integration"—**integrated circuit** technology that allows the equivalent of hundreds of transistors to be crammed into a single chip. See the chart at **chip**.

MTBF "Mean (i.e., average) time between failures"—a measure of the reliability of a piece of hardware.

MTTR "Mean (i.e., average) time to repair"—a measure of how easy a piece of hardware is to fix.

multipass Refers to running through the same data (or some modification of it) more than once, to achieve a goal too complicated to be accomplished in one pass.

A **multipass printer** is a kind of dot-matrix printer that can go back and overstrike text to produce more fully formed, readable characters.

(to) multiplex To interweave two (or more) separate messages on one channel or line, so that they're transmitted simultaneously.

multitasking Doing more than one job at a time; for example, editing one file while printing out another.

multiuser Allowing more than one person to use a computer at the same time.

mumble {hacker jargon} Used when you don't want to go into a whole, long, detailed explanation that the person you're talking to probably wouldn't understand anyway. Novice user: *So the operating system is really sort of a big box that all the other programs go into, right?* Hacker: *Well, mumble.*

(to) mung (pronounced munj by some, but mung by most) {hacker jargon} To make large-scale—usually irrevocable—changes. By extension, to destroy accidentally. *I'm afraid I've munged this whole disk.*

Murphy's Law "If something can go wrong, it will." This law is not exclusive to computer science, of course, but there's probably no other field where it operates with such an implacable vengeance.

My favorite corollary to Murphy's Law is this one: "The first half of any job takes 90% of the time allotted; the second half takes the other 90% of the time." This applies to all programming (without exception) and to all writing too.

N

n (en) Some number to be specified. Often used to represent the **value** of a **parameter**. *To set the left margin, you use the command LMn (where n is the number of spaces you want in the margin).*

Hackers have extended n to mean "some large but indeterminate number." *There were n ways to implement that feature.*

Another hacker meaning for n is "a number that's obvious from the context." The **Jargon File** gives this example: *We'd like to order n wonton soups and a family dinner for n−1* (n minus one)—that is, a wonton soup for everybody at the table and a family dinner for everybody except one.

nanosecond (NAN-oh-) A billionth of a second. Compare **millisecond, microsecond** and **picosecond**.

natural language A language that has evolved more or less without conscious intervention, by means of people speaking it for many years; English, Armenian and Tagalog are three examples. As opposed to artificial, invented languages like Esperanto, Loglan and all the programming languages.

See the diagram and explanation at **programming language**.

NCC The National Computer Conference—a big computer trade show held every year around June.

near-letter-quality Said of **dot-matrix printers** whose output looks almost—but not quite—as good as that produced by **letter-quality printers**. Already a vague term at best, it's sure to become further degraded in time, until it means little more than "legible." In my opinion, "near-letter-quality" should only be applied to matrixes containing a hundred dots or more.

network The connection between several computers or computer devices (like **terminals**). One speaks of being "on"—not "in"—a network. *Which network do you have your account on?* Also see **local network**.

nibble Four **bits**; half a **byte**.

night mode {hacker jargon} Staying up all night and sleeping most of the day—the mode favored by many hackers. *A meeting at 10 a.m.! Are you kidding? I've been in the night mode for weeks.*

Also see **day mode**.

nil {hacker jargon} No. Often used in response to a question using **-p**. As opposed to **T**.

In **Pascal** and some other languages, "nil" means "empty."

no-break space In word processing, when you're dealing with names like B.C. Puckett, V.I. Lenin, Louis IX and WW III, you don't ever want the first part of the name to appear at the end of one line and the second half at the next line. (It looks stupid.)

So some word processing programs give you an option: instead of putting a regular space between V.I. and Lenin, you can put a no-break space (sometimes also called a **hard space**). The words on either side of a no-break space always appear on the same line; no-break spaces will not let themselves be split over the end of lines.

noise Electromagnetic interference, caused by electrical engines, fluorescent lights, television sets, or even components inside the computer itself. Noise can seriously interfere with a computer's operation.

nonemitter Refers to any technology for displaying information that doesn't shine with its own light. **LCD** is one example. Opposite of **phosphorescent**.

nonimpact printers Printers (usually **dot-matrix**) that produce images chemically, thermally or electrostatically, rather than by impact through an inked ribbon. Compare **impact printer**.

number-crunching Tedious, repetitive data processing. In number-crunching, each operation is trivial, but there are lots and lots of operations. Sometimes just called **crunching**.

numeric (noo-MARE-ik) Containing just numbers. As opposed to **alphanumeric**.

numeric keypad Ten number keys arranged in a rectangle, the way they are on a calculator or on your telephone (unless you still live in the Dark Ages and have one of those funny old phones with a round "dial").

O

OASIS (oh-AY-sis) A time-sharing **operating system** developed by Phase One Systems.

object code The output from an **assembler** or **compiler**—all ready (or almost all ready) to be fed to the computer for execution. Object code is always in **machine language**. Compare **source code**. Also see **code**. And see the diagram and explanation at **programming language**.

obscure {hacker jargon} Used in exaggeration of its normal sense, to mean totally incomprehensible. *The cause of that bug is obscure.*

obtw {hacker jargon} An abbreviation for "oh, by the way"—widely used to save time and effort in typed conversations on computer terminals. Also written **btw**.

OCR "Optical character recognition"—any technique by which a computer **peripheral** directly reads typed or printed material.

    The device that actually does the reading is called—not surprisingly—an **OCR reader**. A type font specially designed to be read by such a device is called an **OCR font**.

OEM An "original equipment manufacturer"; actually, a company that assembles computer systems using components many (or all) of which were manufactured by other companies. A better name for this is **system integrator**.

    As opposed to **end users,** who don't resell what they buy.

off-line Not actively connected to a computer (usually said of something that *could* be connected to a computer, but isn't currently). For example, when a printer is off-line it will receive data from its own keyboard, but not from the computer it's hooked up to. (Often printers have switches that let you control whether they're off-line or **on-line**.)

on-line Actively connected to a computer. For example, when a printer is on-line, it's set up to receive data from a computer, rather than from its own keyboard. On-line documentation appears on the screen, rather than in a manual. The opposite is **off-line**.

on-screen formatting In word processing, showing on the screen how a piece of text will look on paper. Actually, much of what's called "on-screen formatting" gives only the sketchiest indication of how text will actually look when printed out.

(to) open (a file) To give a program you're running access to it. For example, if you were doing word processing, you'd have to open a file before you could edit it. (Typically the program will ask you, "Which file do you want to open?")

You can also *create* a file by opening it; you just think up a file name, open an empty file with that name, and start putting stuff in it.

operating system The basic, underlying program that tells your computer what to do and interfaces it with you, the user. Some operating systems work with many different machines, others are specific to just one or two.

Often abbreviated **OS** or **DOS** (for "disk operating system"). Thus the TRS-80 operating system is called **TRSDOS**.

orphan The first line of a paragraph sitting alone at the bottom of a page of text. Some word processing programs know how to suppress orphans. Also see **widow**.

OS Abbreviation for **operating system.** Also abbreviated **DOS.**

OS-9 A multitasking **operating system** that runs on machines built around the 6809 chip.

outdent In word processing, a line of text (usually the first) which extends farther to the left than other lines in the same paragraph. Also called a **hanging indent.** Outdents are used mostly in outlines or lists.

output Data after it's been processed by a computer.

To output is to transfer this data to a printer or storage device.

overlay A piece of a program that sits on the disk until the main part of the program calls it—or a portion of it—into action. At that point it's transferred to some area of **memory** that was already in use and supplants another piece of the program which was sitting there.

overstriking In word processing, printing two or more characters in the same place—as you would to create a ¢ sign for example (if you didn't have another way to do it). Another use for overstriking is in legal documents, where you want to show what text has been deleted: ~~as often as requested~~.

A third use for overstriking is foreign accents. For example, to produce a word like "rêve," you overstrike the e with a ^. (It doesn't look like overstriking because the e and the ^ don't get in each other's way.)

Overstriking is also used to produce slightly bolder text than normal. In this case, each letter is overstruck by itself, either once or several times. This is called **overprinting** or **doublestriking.** Some word processing programs use overprinting to produce **boldfacing,** but **shadow printing** produces a much darker, bolder effect.

P

-p (pee) {hacker jargon} This is put at the end of questions, in imitation of a convention in the **LISP** programming language. In spoken English -p isn't needed, of course, since the rising inflection does the job, but it does add a certain panache. Hacker X: *Food-p?* Hacker Y: *Yeah, good idea. How about the Thai restaurant?*

The Jargon File gives a wonderful example. Bill Gosper wanted to know if someone would share a two-person bowl of wonton soup with him. So naturally he asked: *Split-p soup?* Also see **nil** and **T.**

page Although this word has a technical, computer meaning, it's more often used in computer ads as a rough measure of how much memory or disk storage a particular system has. Since there is no such thing as a standard page, I can only tell you that a regular 8½-by-11 page of double-spaced pica text with 1" margins all around contains about 250 words, or 1½K (see **word** for a discussion of how long the average word actually is).

The same page single-spaced (with blank lines between each paragraph) will average around 400 words (2½K). If you use a lot of short paragraphs when you write, the count can come down as low as 200 words (1¼K) for double-spaced or 300 words (1¾K) for single-spaced. Elite type (twelve characters to the inch) increases all these K values by about 20%.

paper tape An old-fashioned kind of **storage device** that records data in the form of holes punched in a continuous strip of paper.

parallel interface An **interface** on which several bits of data travel over separate wires simultaneously, next to each other.

parameter (puh-RAM-it-er) Something that can be varied but that remains constant in a given context. For example, a formatting parameter is any aspect of a printout that can be changed but that typically stays the same throughout any one printout, for one kind of text, or for a particular file—like the margins, for example, or like the number of characters to the inch. Also see **n**.

PARC See **Xerox PARC**.

parity One of the simplest ways of checking for errors caused by **glitches,** etc. The first seven **bits** of each **byte** carry the information, but the eighth one (called the **parity bit**) checks the other seven. It works something like this:

If there are an odd number of 1s in the byte, the parity bit is 1; if there are an even number, the parity bit is 0. (Some systems reverse this convention; it doesn't really matter which way you do it.) If any of the bits in the byte "fails," the parity bit will also change—either from 1 to 0 or from 0 to 1. (Of course if *two* bits in the same byte fail simultaneously, the parity bit will stay the same, but the odds against this happening are astronomical.)

It's sort of like the way the numbers racket uses the "handle"—the last three numbers of the total amount of bets handled each day at the track (and published on the sports page)—as the daily number; any single, seemingly inconsequential bet will change it. (See **binary numbers, bit** and **byte** for more background.)

(to) parse {hacker jargon} Speaking of fish, to debone. Speaking of anything else, to understand. Hacker X: *I don't like parsing fish.* Hacker Y: *I can parse that.*

Pascal, Blaise (1623–62) French mathematical genius and religious philosopher who, among many other things, invented the first adding machine (called **Pascal's calculator**).

COURTESY OF INTERNATIONAL BUSINESS MACHINES CORPORATION

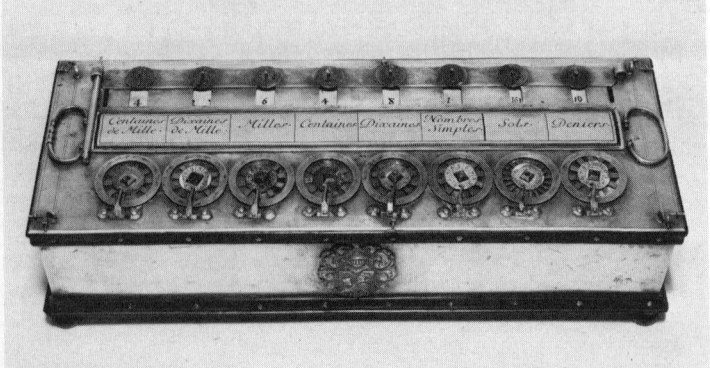

Pascal's calculator   COURTESY OF INTERNATIONAL BUSINESS MACHINES CORPORATION

Pascal A **high-level programming language,** said to be one of the most logical and least **klugy.** (Named after Blaise, of course.) **UCSD Pascal** is one popular variant.

Although Pascal is not an acronym, it's sometimes written all caps: **PASCAL**.

pass One run through the data. Some programs make several passes through the data before they output the results to you. *The Micom 2001 can search for and replace up to 94 different strings in one pass.*

password On multiuser systems, a secret word (or other **string** of characters) you type in to make sure only you (or some other authorized person) can use your account. Since **log-in names** aren't secret, only the password stops someone from telling the system they're you and charging a zillion dollars' worth of computer time to your account.

path In the computers **UNIX** runs on, there are many places to store programs and files. The path tells the **shell** where to look for the programs and files you want to use.

patch A piece of **code** inserted into a program to fix a bug or change something.

PC "Printed circuit"—as in **PC board**.

PC is also a common nickname for the IBM Personal Computer, or for any personal computer.

PCB An extremely deadly group of chemicals that have been spilled just about everywhere, thanks to the general trustworthiness of U.S. industry and our reluctance to "over-regulate" it.

In the world of computers, PCB stands for **printed circuit board**.

PC DOS A CP/M-like operating system for the IBM Personal Computer, developed for IBM by MicroSoft. Also called **MDOS, MSDOS, IBM DOS** and—by IBM itself—simply **DOS**.

PDP-8, -10, -11, etc. A widely used line of **DEC minicomputers.** PDP stands for "programmable digital processor."

peripheral Any device connected to a computer—e.g., a monitor, keyboard, printer, terminal, etc.

permanent storage A synonym for **storage**.

personal computer A microcomputer designed to be used primarily by one person (usually—but not necessarily—its owner).

some personal computers

personalized form letters Generated by a **merge-print program,** each of these is more or less identical to every other, but personalizing data (like the name of the addressee, where s/he lives, how much s/he owes, etc.) is inserted into each one. The program gets this personal information from a mailing list, from a data file, or directly from the computer operator while the letter is being printed out.

phantom {hacker jargon} What a **dragon** is called at **SAIL**.

phosphor The stuff on the inside of a CRT that glows when the electron beam hits it. It continues to glow for a moment, giving the picture a bit of permanence. Also see **high-persistence phosphor**.

pica (PIE-kuh) In typesetting, a sixth of an inch. More commonly used to refer to **pica type**—a size which fits ten characters into each horizontal inch. Compare **elite type**.

picosecond (PEE-koh-SEH-kund) A trillionth of a second. Compare **millisecond, microsecond** and **nanosecond**.

pins The small metal connectors on a **DIP** that fit into sockets on a **board**.

pin-compatible Said of chips which perform the same functions and can be substituted for one another.

pin feed Pins, set at either end of the platen, which engage sprocket holes on the edge of **continuous form paper** to pull it through the printer. Compare **tractor feed** and **friction feed**.

PIP (pronounced as a word, not as three letters) A **CP/M** utility program, used most frequently for copying files from one disk to another. The name stands for "peripheral interchange program."

(to) pipe In **UNIX**, to transfer data from one program to another, so that the output of the first program becomes the input of the second. *Pipe the text to the line printer to check it out; then when you have it right, pipe it to the typesetter.*

pixel One of the little dots of light that make up the picture on a **CRT**. The more pixels there are, the higher the **resolution**.

PL/1 A **high-level programming language** developed for the **IBM 360 series** in the mid-'60s; it's designed to handle both business and scientific applications. The name stands for "programming language 1." Also see **PL/M**.

plasma See **gas plasma**.

PL/M A **high-level programming language** derived from PL/1, developed by Gary Kildall for Intel to run on computers smaller than **IBM 360s**. The name stands for "programming language for microprocessors." Also see **SPL/M**.

plotter A computer **peripheral** that draws things.

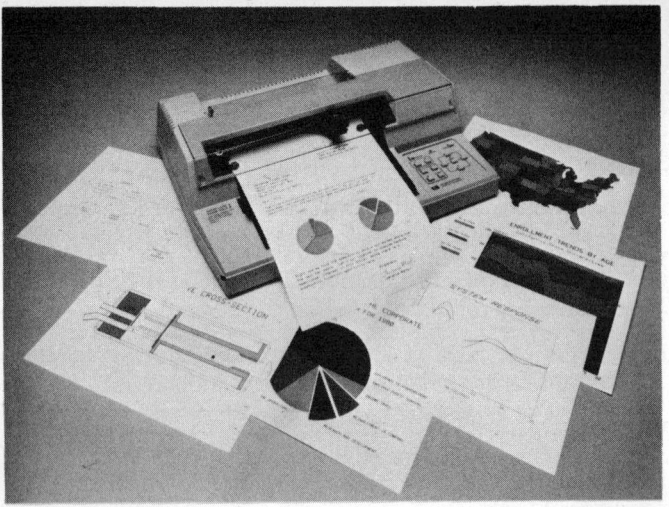

a plotter and its output COURTESY OF HEWLETT-PACKARD

plug-compatible Said of components that can be substituted for each other without any modification of the system.

pointer An **address** that tells a program where to find something.

pointing-finger syndrome A situation where two different suppliers of computer products each blame the other for a problem. This most often comes up when a hardware manufacturer says the software is at fault and the software publisher says the hardware is at fault.

GAR SMITH

Polish notation A system of arithmetical notation developed by the Polish logician Jan Lukasiewicz. First you enter the numbers, then you say what you're going to do to them. Thus 2 + 2 is written 2, 2 +. Polish notation is used in the **Forth** programming language and on most HP calculators. Sometimes called "reverse Polish notation."

POM-dependent {hacker jargon} Dependent on the *p*hase *of* the *m*oon—that is, flaky, not dependable.

(to) **popj** (POP-jay) {hacker jargon} To return from a digression. To **pop the stack** is also heard.
   Popj popj (or simply **pop pop**) is more or less equivalent to "Now let's see, where was I?" (From an instruction used on the **PDP-10**.) Compare **pushj**.

port A sweet wine that ... uh, no, *here* it means a place to connect other devices to a computer. Also called an **I/O** (input/output) **port**. I/O ports can be **serial** or **parallel**. Also called a **jack**.

power supply The device that converts the 110/120-volt AC electricity from your wall socket to DC electricity of the proper voltage for use by a computer, printer, etc. The name is a little confusing, since power supplies don't supply power, but only modify it.

pph "Pages per hour."

print head The part of a printer that actually puts the image on paper. It sometimes contains a removable **print element.**

print element On **formed-character printers,** the removable part of the **print head.** (It's removable so you can change the type style.) The two main kinds of print elements are **daisy wheels** and **thimbles.**

printed circuit board A **board** on which the chips are connected by circuits printed with metallic ink, rather than by wires. Usually called a **PC board.**

printer A computer **peripheral** that produces hard copies of text on paper. The term is a little confusing, since what printers do is actually much closer to typing than printing—that is, they don't set type or produce anything that would normally be called "printed matter."

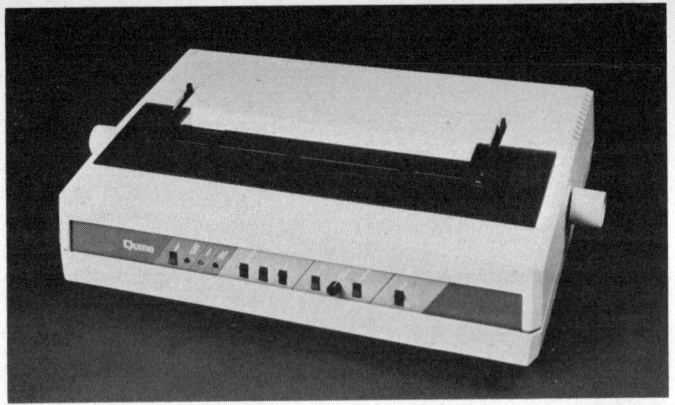
a formed-character printer COURTESY OF QUME CORPORATION—A SUBSIDIARY OF ITT

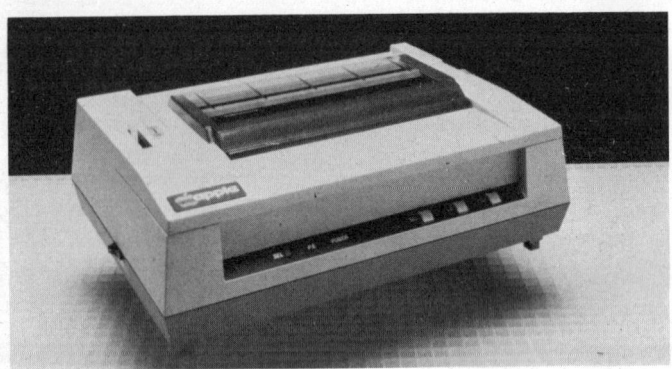
a dot-matrix printer COURTESY OF APPLE COMPUTERS, INC.

printer terminal A keyboard and printer combination, capable of being connected to a computer. As distinguished from a **VDT**.

printout A **hard copy** of computer data, prepared on a printer. **To print out** is to produce such a copy.

print-time commands Formatting commands that are given to the word processing program right before you print out a file (as opposed to **embedded commands**).

private data base See **data base**.

processor-bound Refers to processes or programs that are slowed down by the amount of time it takes the **CPU** to do the actual computing—that is, the **I/O** devices have to sit around and twiddle their thumbs waiting for the CPU to finish. As opposed to **I/O-bound.**

program A set of instructions that tells a computer what to do. Also called **software.**

There are three main types of programs:

—**systems software,** which includes **operating systems, programming languages** and **utility programs;**

—**applications programs,** which include software that does accounting, word processing, data management, communications, graphics and the like; and

—**learning programs and games,** which include ... uh ... learning programs and games.

programmable function key A key whose function varies with the software you're using.

programmer Someone who uses a programming language to write programs. As opposed to a **user.** Also see **systems analyst.**

programming language A tool for writing programs, an artificial language for communicating with computers—as opposed to the **natural languages** (like English) that people use to communicate with each other. Programming languages occupy a middle ground between **machine language** (the actual **instructions** computers understand) and human speech.

There are two basic kinds of programming languages—high-level and assembly. **High-level languages** are closer to natural language and usually work on several different kinds of machines. They're generally easier to program in but produce slower-running programs. **COBOL, Pascal** and **FORTRAN** are three examples. (Although some people call them **low-level languages, BASIC** and **Forth** are also high-level languages for the purposes of this explanation.)

Assembly languages are a mnemonic form of machine language and only work with one particular kind of **CPU chip** (in fact, they're named for the chip they work with—"6502 assembly language", for example). They're generally harder to program in but produce faster-running programs (in the hands of a competent programmer).

The diagram on the next page looks complicated at first because it incorporates a lot of information. But don't be

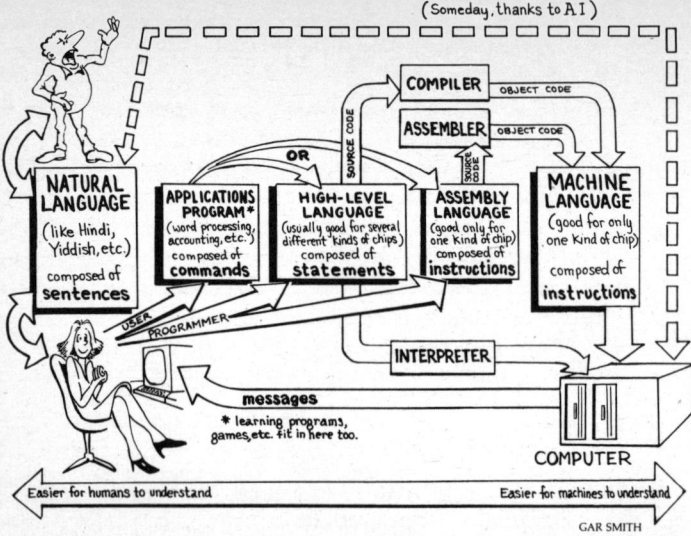

intimidated by it; after I've walked you through it, you'll see how it all makes sense.

The different kinds of languages are arranged across the middle. The farther to the left a language is, the easier it is for a human being to understand; the farther to the right, the easier for a computer to understand. Someday the science of **artificial intelligence** will advance to the point where computers and people can talk directly to each other (that's what the dotted line is about). But for the time being, we have to use intermediaries.

The simplest of these intermediaries for a computer novice to deal with is an **applications program, learning program** or game (which aren't really languages at all). Applications programs help you do particular practical tasks—like writing and editing text, or doing your taxes. They're written in programming languages, by **programmers.** (People who use applications programs but don't write ones of their own are called **users.**)

Next simplest are the high-level languages. Unlike applications programs, which are composed of **commands,** high-level languages are composed of **statements.** (The difference is that a command executes as soon as you give it, but statements only execute when you run the program.)

When a programmer has finished writing all the statements in a high-level program, this **source code** either gets executed directly by an **interpreter** or translated into **object code** by a compiler (see **compiler** for more on the difference between them).

Assembly language is made up of instructions rather than statements (**instructions** tell the computer to do just one thing; statements are more complex). The program that translates assembly-language source code into object code is called an **assembler**.

When the computer talks to you, whether in response to a command you've given in an applications program or a statement in a programming language, what it tells you is called a **message**.

And that's all there is to it. Not as easy to follow as prime-time television perhaps, but understandable all the same.

PROM (prahm) A "programmable read-only memory." It tells the computer what to do, and you can only change it with a piece of hardware called a **PROM programmer**. It usually comes as a **DIP**, and is referred to as *a* PROM.

prompt A symbol on the screen that tells you the computer is ready for you to tell it what to do next. Each program has its own distinctive prompt—a dash, an underline, the percent sign, a star or whatever.

Sometimes prompts are messages that guide you through a process. For example, a mailing list program might provide the following prompts to help you enter data: NAME? ADDRESS? CITY? and so on.

proofing program Another name for a **spelling checker**.

(true) **proportional spacing** Proportional spacing is the main thing that makes something that's typeset easier to read than something that's typed.

In normal typing, all letters get the same space, regardless of how wide or narrow they are. For example, look at the word `commission` when it's typed. Because the *m*'s are wider than the average letter, they look squeezed together. Because the *i*'s are narrower than most letters, they look like they're floating alone. The *co, ss* and *on* look OK, because *c*'s, *s*'s, *o*'s and *n*'s are of average width. Capitalization makes the situation even more extreme. A capital *M* or *W* is *much* wider than a small *i* or *l*.

Proportional spacing takes the varying widths of letters into account and gives each character exactly the width it needs—no more, no less. Compare the word commission when it's typeset. The *m*'s get more room and the *i*'s get less.

Some word processing programs can produce proportional spacing (when used with printers that have **microspacing**). Because proportional spacing involves a lot of computation, the software that does it takes a lot of memory; for this reason, it's sometimes put into a separate program from the word processing program, or into an **overlay**.

I refer to "true" proportional spacing because some word processing programs claim to have proportional spacing when all they really have is **microjustification**.

proprietary Belonging to just one company, and not widely used outside of that company (e.g., a proprietary chip).

protocol A set of procedures that controls how information is transmitted between computers. *Yeah, both these machines communicate synchronously, but they use different protocols.*

p-System See **UCSD p-System**.

public data base See **data base**.

(to) punt {hacker jargon} To give up. (From football, of course).

punched card A card on which data is stored by means of holes punched into it. The most common kind is the **Hollerith card**.

(to) pushj (pusii jay) {hacker jargon} To begin a digression (from an instruction used on the **PDP-10**). Compare **popj**.

Q

ques (kwess) {hacker jargon} A spoken abbreviation for "question mark." Also called **what**.

queue (kyoo) The only common word in the English language with four vowels in a row (except for "queueing," which has five).

In the world of computers, a queue is a bunch of things waiting, in order, to be processed by a computer or a **peripheral.** *We might as well go see a movie or something. The printer queue is so long, your file isn't going to get printed out for hours.*

FIFO and **LIFO** are two common kinds of queues.

QWERTY (KWIR-tee) The standard layout for keyboards, where the leftmost letter keys on the second line are q, w, e, r, t and y, and where you can spell "typewriter" with the keys on that line.

QWERTY was actually *designed* to be clumsy. The inventors of the first commercial typewriter (Sholes, Soulé and Glidden) had a problem with keys jamming. So they played with different arrangements of the keys (which were originally in alphabetical order) until they happened upon QWERTY; it was so inconvenient that virtually no one could type fast enough to jam the keys, no matter how hard s/he tried. (What the hell—it was easier than improving the machine.)

Newer, more efficient keyboards have actually been *designed to be easy to use* (what a concept!). See **Dvorak keyboard** and the illustration at **keyboard.**

R

ragged left An unusual format in which the right margin is straight but the left is uneven. Also see **justification.**

ragged right The normal format for typewritten text. The left margin is straight but the right is uneven. Also see **justification.**

RAM (pronounced as in "battering ram") "Random-access memory." Actually, most sorts of memory are randomly accessed, but the term "RAM" has come to mean what is more correctly called **read/write memory**—that is, memory you can both write data into and read data out of (as opposed to **ROM**).

The amount of RAM a computer has is an important measure of its usefulness, because RAM is where you do all your work. Whatever is in RAM disappears when you turn the computer off (except on a few unusual computers). Also see **memory**.

R&D (are-un-DEE) "Research and development"—an important division (and activity) of most computer firms.

the RAND Corporation A private research center in Santa Monica, California, that does a lot of work for the government, particularly in the area of computers. The name comes from "*r*esearch *an*d *d*evelopment."

random {hacker jargon} Hackers use this word in both its ordinary sense (haphazard, patternless)—*The system's been behaving pretty randomly*—and to mean something like "typically worthless"—as in *random loser* or *random hacker*. The **Jargon File** gives this example: Hacker X: *Who was at the conference?* Hacker Y: *Just a bunch of random business types.*

The expression **J. Random** is also used (in imitation of J. Fred Muggs, who—I suppose—could be called J. Random Chimpanzee, except that he was rather exceptional). *Should J. Random Loser be allowed to tie up the system all day working on his term paper?* See **bogus** for a list of synonyms.

random access A method of **accessing** data where each piece of information is retrieved directly by means of its **address**, independently of any other piece of information. As opposed to **sequential** (or **serial**) **access.**

An everyday analogy to random access is putting a phonograph needle down on a record. You can put it on any track of the record, regardless of what songs come before or after the one you want. Sequential access is like finding a song on a tape. You have to fast-forward or reverse past other songs on the tape to get to the one you want; you can't access it directly.

For most applications, random access is far superior to sequential access.

(to) rape {hacker jargon} To violently damage or destroy something. *Some random hacker managed to rape the master directory.*

(to) **rave** {hacker jargon} In addition to its normal meaning (which it shares with **flame**), rave is used by hackers to refer to friendly bullshitting. *We raved all night about this and that.*

(to) **read** To absorb information from a disk or other storage medium. Compare with **write**.

read-only Only capable of being **read**, not **written** to—like disks that are **write-protected**, or read-only memory (**ROM**). Abbreviated **R/O**.

read/write Capable of both absorbing and depositing information, or capable of having information absorbed from it and deposited on it—for example, **read/write memory** (see **RAM**) and **read/write head** (see **head**). As opposed to **read-only**.

real-time Said of computer functions that happen fast enough to keep up with whatever they're controlling or responding to. **Interactive** programs like airline reservation systems are real-time because they tell you how much space is left on a plane at any given moment, and change those figures the instant you enter your reservation.

Another kind of real-time program is one that monitors a manufacturing process and responds immediately to variations in temperature, pH or whatever. As opposed to **batch processing**. Also see **real-time clock**.

real-time clock An actual clock (in the usual sense of the word). Real-time clocks are used in computers to automatically put the date and time on documents and to indicate when a file was last revised. On multiuser systems, they keep track of how long each individual user has been working (for billing purposes). Also see **clock**.

real users {hacker jargon} People who actually pay for the computer time they use, and/or who use a computer to write papers, to do course work and for other concrete projects. As opposed to **hackers**, who generally use the computer for free and see working with it as an end in itself. Also see **user**.

the **real world** {hacker jargon} Any place populated by non-hackers; that dim shadow-world of suits and ties, 9 to 5, and business programming. *Poor fellow, he left MIT and went out into the real world* (to be said in approximately the same tone as *Poor fellow, dying like that, right at his prime*).

reboot To dump whatever you're working on and **boot** the operating system again. Also called a **warm start** or **warm boot**.

record A relatively small collection of related pieces of information. For example, in a mailing list program, the name, address, city, state, zip code, phone number and other data on one particular person or company. Also see **data base**.

reference card A small card designed to be propped up near the keyboard which lists the commands in a particular program.

reference manual A manual designed to be referred to after a program (or computer system) has been more or less learned. Compare **training manual**.

refresh rate How frequently something is electronically **rewritten**. A common refresh rate for the image on a screen is 30 times a second; a common refresh rate for the contents of **dynamic** memory is 500 times a second.

register A small piece of memory right in the **CPU chip** that can be accessed very quickly. The CPU uses it to temporarily store a piece of data while it's computing something.

release version The version of a program that's sold to the public.

report What a printout of the processed data is called under most kinds of programs.

(to) reset To flush memory, thereby throwing out whatever programs, text, etc. had been loaded into it. Sometimes the operating system is automatically reloaded (**rebooted**) when you reset, sometimes not.

On some systems, reset is accomplished by using both hands to hold down two or three keys simultaneously. On others, there's a special **reset button**.

The safest place for a reset button is on the computer **box**, as far from the keyboard as possible. On computers where the keyboard and computer are all one piece, the reset button should be on the back, somewhere hard to reach (or, better, should require a combination of keys). Much wailing and gnashing of **teeth** has been caused by reset buttons that were accidentally hit.

resolution The number of little dots in a character, or on a screen. The more there are, the more fine detail there will be (**high resolution**); the fewer there are, the grosser and clumsier the image will be (**low resolution**).

By the way, don't confuse the size of a **CRT** with its resolution. On a big screen with low resolution, the dots (**pixels**) are just bigger.

RETURN A key found on most computer keyboards. Its function varies with the software, but it's typically used to enter commands and/or to do what the equivalent key on a typewriter keyboard does—move you to the beginning of the next line. Sometimes the RETURN key is labeled **ENTER;** on the IBM PC, it's marked with a left-curving arrow. Also see **carriage return.**

reverse video Dark letters on a light background, as opposed to the usual light-on-dark CRT image.

(to) rewrite To redeposit information. *You won't be bothered with flicker on this CRT, because it rewrites the screen sixty times a second.*

rewrite flicker On systems that operate in **terminal mode** with relatively slow **baud rates,** the flickering of the screen caused by the image changing.

rigid disk Another name for a **hard disk.**

R/O (also **RO**) "Receive-only." Usually refers to a printer without a keyboard, which can only do what the computer tells it to do and can't send information back to the computer. Compare **KSR.**

Also, an abbreviation for **read-only.**

ROM (rahm) "Read-only memory." It tells the computer what to do, but you can't change what it says (as opposed to **RAM**). ROM usually comes in the form of a **DIP,** which is referred to as *a* ROM or as a ROM chip. Also see **memory.**

rotary control knob A circular device, mounted on some Hewlett-Packard keyboards, that moves the cursor when you press down on its edge. Also see **CAT, mouse** and **trackball.**

routine Any piece of **code** (up to and including a whole program) which performs one particular job. There are two basic kinds: main routines and subroutines. **Subroutines** are always called up by other routines and tend to be used more than once in one program. One subroutine can call a second subroutine which can call a third subroutine and so on *ad infinitum,* but there is only one **main routine** in each program.

Route 128 Silicon Valley East; eastern Massachusetts and southern New Hampshire, where there's a large concentration of computer companies (Route 128 encircles the greater Boston area).

RPG A **high-level programming language** developed at IBM, mostly used in business applications. The name stands for "report program generator."

RS-232 An industry-standard **serial interface** set up by the **EIA**, a trade association of electronics manufacturers. Unfortunately, "industry-standard" is something of a hoax in this case. Manufacturers make interfaces just about any damn way they please and call them RS-232; after they're sold, who cares if people can connect other companies' equipment to them? It serves the public right for buying from another manufacturer.

RS stands for "recommended standard." Also see **connector conspiracy** and **industry-standard.**

rude {hacker jargon} Said of a program which is badly written and hard to use.

(x) **runs on** (y) X program will function on y machine.

(x) **runs under** (y) In order for x program to function, y program must have first been loaded into the machine.

R/W Abbreviation for **read/write.**

S

S-100 bus A common microcomputer **bus** originally developed by and for hobbyists and now found on many different brands of machines. (Not to be confused with the M-100 bus—you can tell them apart because the S-100 doesn't turn left on 125th Street.)

sacred {hacker jargon} Reserved for the exclusive use of something or someone. *This portion of memory is sacred to the BIOS.*

SAIL The Stanford Artificial Intelligence Laboratory at Stanford University in Palo Alto, California—an important center of computer research. Also see **computer science.**

save To copy a **file** from **RAM** to **disk** (or to some other storage medium). If you don't save a file, you'll lose it when you turn the computer off.

Schottky (SHOT-key) A certain kind of high-speed circuit.

screen The most common way of referring to a **monitor** or a **display.**

screen editor A type of **editor** that lets you move the cursor all around the screen (as opposed to a **line editor**).

screenful The amount of data that fits on the screen. Obviously, how much data is in a screenful varies with the system.

screen update Changing of the screen to reflect new information (despite the use of the word "date," it happens in a fraction of a second).

scrolling Looking at a file that's longer than a screenful by moving it past the screen (usually vertically, unless **horizontal scrolling** is specified).

    Automatic scrolling is moving through the text without having to keep holding a key down (you give one command and the data just keeps scrolling past until you tell it to stop).

sec or **sec . . .** {hacker jargon} Abbreviations for "wait a second"—widely used to save time and effort in typed conversations on computer terminals.

secondary memory Another name for **storage**. Also called **secondary storage**.

second generation Computers that used transistors for their switches. (Some people refer to these as third-generation computers and call the second generation those computers—like ENIAC and UNIVAC—that used vacuum tubes as their switches.) See the chart at **fourth generation.**

sector Data is stored on disks in concentric **tracks** (sort of like the grooves on a phonograph record, but not connected with each other). Each of these tracks is divided into several sectors. Thus each sector is shaped like a portion of a circle. On a floppy disk, a sector typically contains between 128 and 512 **bytes.**

semiconductor An electronic device that takes advantage of the fact that certain materials, like silicon and germanium, conduct electricity less well than metals but better than insulators. When impurities like phosphorus or arsenic are added to these materials, they can be made to act like transistors and other devices. (Explaining exactly how this is done would only confuse you—as well as me.)

All **chips** are semiconductors (except for carrot chips, which conduct electricity so well they can be substituted for copper wire).

semi-immediately {hacker jargon} Probably within two or three years. Hacker X: *When is the system coming up?* Hacker Y: *Semi-immediately.*

sequential access A method of **accessing** data which requires that you go past other pieces of information to get to the one you want. See **random access** for more information.

serial access Another name for **sequential access.**

serial interface An **interface** on which all the data moves over the same wire, one bit after the other.

service contract You pay a certain amount per year (or per month) and if anything goes wrong with the hardware, they fix it for free.

shadow printing Printing a character, moving right a tiny bit, and printing it again (and possibly repeating that process several times). Only printers with **microspacing** can do shadow printing.

Shannon test (or **text**) A piece of text designed to determine the speed of a printer in actual use, as opposed to its **burst speed.** Developed by Claude Shannon (1916–), "the father of information theory."

shared-logic More than one terminal connected to one computer. Also see **logic.**

shared-resource More than one computer connected to one printer, disk drive, or other expensive peripheral.

shell The part of the **UNIX operating system** that's responsible for the **user interface** (among other things). It's the shell that gives different versions of UNIX their different flavors.

As the illustration indicates, the shell gets its name from the fact that it surrounds the computer and the other parts of the operating system, so that the user never sees them directly.

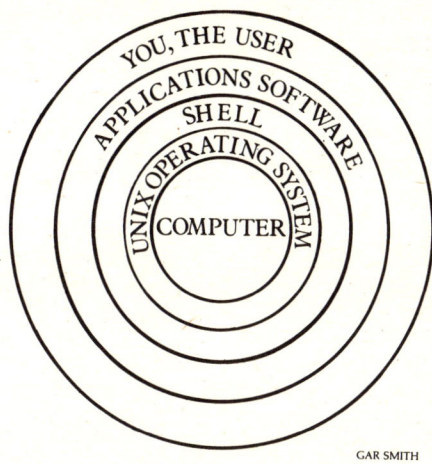
GAR SMITH

silicon A chemical element (atomic number 14) widely found in sand and clay. Silicon is used in the manufacture of glass, pottery, concrete, brick and—more to the point—**integrated circuits.** (See **chip** for details.)

silicone One of several compounds made from **silicon** and other ingredients. Silicone has nothing to do with computers, but people sometimes get confused and talk about "Silicone Valley" and the like.

Silicon Valley (don't call it *the* Silicon Valley, and especially not Silicon*e* Valley) The Santa Clara valley, at the southern end of San Francisco Bay.

Once famous for its fruit orchards, this beautiful, tranquil dale had the bad—or good—luck (depending on how you look at it) to contain Stanford University, which fathered forth the **semiconductor**—and therefore also the computer—industry. Now the orchards are gone and Silicon Valley—so called because silicon is used in computer chips—is crammed full of high-tech corporations and overpriced houses.

SILICON VALLEY—1940's   GAR SMITH

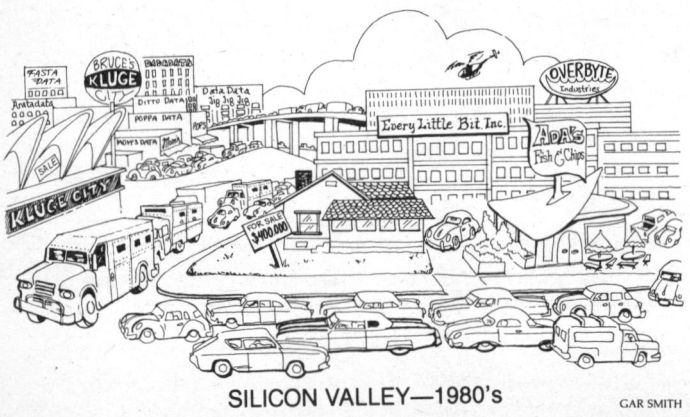
SILICON VALLEY—1980's   GAR SMITH

The major towns in Silicon Valley are Sunnyvale, Saratoga, Santa Clara, San Jose, Palo Alto, Mountain View, Milpitas, Menlo Park, Los Gatos, Los Altos, Cupertino and Campbell. Within their borders, a large percentage of all American computer products are designed and built.

simplex Capable of transmitting data in one direction only—that is, either to *or* from a given location. As opposed to **duplex.** Also see **full duplex** and **half duplex.**

simulation Using a computer to imitate or represent some real-life situation, object or process. For example, a computer can simulate the flight of a rocket, taking into account things like crosswinds, the earth's rotation, variations in the rocket's thrust, and so on.

single-board computer A **CPU, memory, clock** and **interfaces** all on a single **board.** Of course it's not a computer in the everyday sense of the word, because it lacks a keyboard, screen, storage device, etc.

single-density The original format for putting information on a floppy disk. It only gives you half as much capacity as **double-density,** but it's somewhat more reliable.

single-sided Refers to floppy disks that store information on only one side.

sixteen-bit chip A **CPU chip** that handles data sixteen bits at a time. The **68000, 8086** and **Z8000** are a few examples.

16 x 64 (the x is pronounced "by") Sixteen lines of 64 characters—a somewhat obsolete format for text on a computer screen. Compare **24 x 80.**

16/32-bit chip A **CPU chip** that handles data in 32-bit chunks internally but takes it in and sends it out sixteen bits at a time. The **68000** is one example.

6502 An **eight-bit chip** made by MOS Technology, used in the Apple II, Atari, Commodore and other computers.

6800 An **eight-bit chip** made by Motorola.

6809 An **8/16-bit chip** made by Motorola that's used in the Radio Shack Color Computer and other machines.

68000 A **16/32-bit chip** made by Motorola that's used in the Apple Lisa and other computers.

(to) slave To make one computer (or component) do only what another computer (or component) tells it to do.

slots The openings in a **motherboard** that **boards** plug into. Also see **expansion slots**.

small-scale integration See **SSI**.

Smalltalk A menu-driven high-level **programming language** developed at **Xerox PARC** in the 1970s and often used in conjunction with a **mouse**.

smart Having a significant amount of computational ability of its own (as opposed to **dumb**). Said of terminals, keyboards, printers, etc. Also see **intelligent**.

smoke test {hacker jargon} Plugging in something you've just finished building, simply to see if it will smoke, blow up or malfunction in some other obvious way. Once it passes the smoke test, you can then go on to see if it actually does what it's supposed to do.

Also used more loosely to refer to the first time you try out any newly developed product (a new program, for example), regardless of whether you actually connect it to electrical power.

GAR SMITH

smooth scrolling The ability to **scroll** text without it jerking from one line to the next.

(to) snarf {hacker jargon} To grab (a file, usually). Sometimes snarf implies you're using the file without the owner's permission.

snivitz {hacker jargon} A small **glitch.**

SNOBOL (sNow-ball) A **high-level programming language** particularly adapted to handling **strings** of symbols. One common application of SNOBOL is translating languages. The name stands for—now get this—"*stri*ng-*o*riented sym*bo*lic *l*anguage"; how's that for stretching?

soft When part of a computer term, "soft" has the general meaning of "changeable." As opposed to **hard.**

SoftCard A **board** that plugs into the Apple II and allows it to run **CP/M,** by **slaving** the Apple's own 6502 **CPU chip** to the Z80 CPU chip on the SoftCard. Also see **Baby Blue.**

soft carriage return A symbol, which usually doesn't show on the screen, that generates a **line feed/carriage return** when it falls at the end of a line, and a space otherwise. As opposed to a **hard carriage return.** Also called a **conditional carriage return.**

soft hyphen This prints as a hyphen when it falls at the end of a line, and disappears when it doesn't fall at the end of a line. As opposed to a **hard hyphen.** Also called a **conditional hyphen.**

soft key A **programmable function key;** what it does varies with the software you're using. Compare **dedicated key.**

soft-sectored Describes a kind of **floppy disk** that lets the **operating system** choose where to record information on it. As opposed to a **hard-sectored** disk, which has a ring of small holes that dictate where the **sectors** go.

software The instructions that tell a computer what to do (as opposed to the actual **hardware**). Also called programs.
For a list of the main kinds of software, see **program.**

software-compatible Said of **CPU chips** that have the same **instruction set** and thus can use the same software. For example, the 8088 is software-compatible with the 8086.

software rot {hacker jargon} A mythical disease of software in which programs stop working (or stop working right) if they aren't used for a long time. Also called **bit decay.**

(I call this a mythical disease because simply not using a program can't actually alter it in any way. Still, hackers report that it happens, for some reason or another.)

softwarily {hacker jargon} In software, or with respect to software. *We decided to implement this feature softwarily.* As opposed to **hardwarily**.

SOS (pronounced sauce, as in "apple sauce") "Sophisticated operating system"—the **operating system** that comes on an Apple III.

source code The **code** a programmer writes. Source code must be run through an **assembler** or **compiler** and turned into **machine language** before a computer can understand it. Unlike **object code,** source code can contain **comments.** Also see **code.** And see the diagram and explanation at **programming language.**

SPACEBAR The official name (all caps) for the long, narrow key at the bottom of keyboards that generates spaces.

(to) spazz {hacker jargon} To behave erratically. *Boy, is he spazzing!* Can also be applied to hardware or software.

spelling checker A program that goes through a file and checks for spelling errors. Sometimes called a **dictionary program.**

spike A sudden, sharp increase in voltage. Also called a **surge.**

splat {hacker jargon} This name is used by hackers for many different symbols. It most often refers to the **star** (*), but it can also refer to the pound sign (#), a circle with an x in it, a circle with a + in it, or other symbols.

split screen A feature that allows you to see more than one piece of text (usually two, but sometimes many) on the screen at the same time. Also see **window.**

SPL/M A **high-level programming language** derived from **PL/M.** SPL/M features extremely fast **compiling** of **code** and is mostly used for **systems software.** The name stands for "systems programming language for microprocessors."

spooling A method for working on files that are larger than the available memory space. Different parts of the **workfile** are loaded into memory at different times and are put back on the disk and replaced with other parts as needed. Also called **swapping** in this sense.

Spooling is also used to edit one file while printing out another in the **background.** This is called **print spooling.**

A device that enables a computer to spool is called a **spooler.** "Spool" stands for "simultaneous peripheral operations on-line."

spreadsheet program See **electronic spreadsheet program**.

SRA Science Research Associates—a Chicago-based research company now owned by IBM. It produces computer learning programs (among other things).

SRI International A computer think tank (among other things) in Palo Alto, California, where the **mouse** (among other things) was developed. The initials stand for (or stood for) Stanford Research Institutes, although SRI is no longer affiliated with Stanford University.

SSI "Small-scale integration"—**integrated circuit** technology that allows the equivalent of up to a hundred transistors to be crammed onto a single chip. See the chart at **chip.**

stand-alone Capable of operating on its own; not needing to be hooked up to other hardware or software. A **stand-alone program** is one that runs independently of an **operating system.**

star What the * symbol is usually called by computer people. The term "asterisk" is much less common. Sometimes * is called **glob** or **splat.** Also see the listing under * at the end of the book.

statement Programs written in **high-level languages** are composed of statements which translate into **instructions** to the machine, and also of **comments** which remind the programmer what the various statements are supposed to do. See the diagram and explanation at **programming language.**

static RAM Memory which, unlike **dynamic RAM,** doesn't need to be **refreshed** (i.e. **rewritten**) many times a second. It's more expensive than dynamic RAM, but is less susceptible to damage from **glitches** and other kinds of **dirty power.**

stoppage (STOP-ij) {hacker jargon} Extreme **lossage** that results in something (usually something vital) becoming completely unusable.

storage The long-term retention of computer information in a relatively easy-to-change form on **magnetic media** like floppy disks, hard disks, cassette tapes, streaming tapes and **bubble memory** boards. Data is read off of and written onto these media by **storage devices** (such as disk drives). See **memory** for a more complete discussion of the distinction between memory and storage.

streaming tape A fast method of storing computer data. A typical tape cartridge operating in "streaming mode" is capable of recording 30,000 **bytes** per second.

string Any specified sequence of characters. A string can be a word, a number, a phrase—whatever. For example, you might specify a string to be searched for, or to be found and replaced with a different string.

subroutine In programming, a subsidiary **routine** that is called (up) by a **main routine** or another subroutine—often more than once in the program.

supercomputer The largest class of computers. Supercomputers are incredibly powerful but, unfortunately, are mostly used for things like weapons research. Compare **microcomputers, minicomputers** and **mainframes**.

support 1. Verbal advice and help with computer problems. Support is usually provided by the vendor that sells you the product, and only secondarily by the manufacturer or publisher of the product. *We support what we sell.*

2. To say a piece of hardware or software "supports" something means that it works with it. *The WRITE word processing program supports just about any terminal.*

The connection between the two meanings is this: computers are so complex that you're crazy to try to make two things work together if someone doesn't promise to help you with any problems that come up. (And don't think you can solve every problem yourself; everybody, no matter how experienced, needs *some* level of support.) *The availability of support is the single most important consideration in buying any computer product.*

support GAR SMITH

support contract You pay money just so you can ask the people who sold you a product questions about it.

surge A sudden, sharp increase in voltage. Also called a **spike.**

surge suppressor A device that evens out surges.

swapping Another name for **spooling** the **workfile.**

symbols Many common symbols (for example, *, . and :) have special meanings in the world of computers. Several of them are listed at the back of the book.

synchronous (SIN-krun-us) Occurring at precisely timed intervals.

   Because the **synchronous transmission** of data doesn't require "start" bits and "stop" bits, it's more efficient than its opposite—asynchronous transmission (see **asynchronous** for more details).

system A computer plus its **peripherals**—terminal, printer, keyboard, monitor, disk drives, etc. Sometimes a system also includes software.

system disk Any disk that has the **operating system** (and often **utilities** and other programs) on it. If a disk isn't a system disk, you can't use it to **boot.** Compare **work disk.**

system integrator A company that assembles computer systems using components most (or all) of which were manufactured by other companies. Usually called an **OEM.**

system reset The name for **resetting** on an IBM Personal Computer. It's accomplished by holding down three keys.

systems analyst Someone who figures out what kind of software is required to meet a given need, then tells a programmer what sort of code needs to be written (often by working up a **flowchart**). Systems analysts were once programmers themselves and are usually glad not to have to actually write code anymore. (On the other hand, on small jobs, they sometimes write the code themselves.)

systems software Software that underlies **applications programs, learning programs** and games and helps them work. The three basic types of systems software are **operating systems, programming languages** and **utilities.**

system unit On an IBM Personal Computer, the computer **box** that contains the **CPU** and memory, as well as the disk drives.

T

T Yes; true. As opposed to **nil.** Often in response to a question using **-p.**

tasteful, tasty {hacker jargon} Said of programs, this means they are written in a clean, efficient manner, without a lot of sloppy patchwork, **hacks** and **kluges. Elegant** is a synonym. Also see **flavorful.**

TECO An **editor** developed at MIT; many other editors are direct or indirect descendants of it. The name stands for "*t*ext *e*ditor and *co*rrector."

terminal A device used to feed information and/or instructions to a computer and to get the same back from it. When it consists of a keyboard and a CRT, it's called a **video terminal** or **VDT;** when it consists of a keyboard and a printer, it's called a **printer terminal.** When the word "terminal" is used without qualification, it almost always means a VDT, since printer terminals are now pretty much obsolete (at least in computer applications).

Terminals vary in terms of how **smart** or **dumb** they are—that is, how much computational ability they have. Also see **console.**

a terminal COURTESY OF HEWLETT-PACKARD

terminal mode A system for transmitting information to the screen by first sending it to the terminal's **character buffer** to be formatted. As opposed to **memory-mapped video.**

text Alphanumeric data.

text editor Another name for an **editor.**

text file A file that contains text (rather than, say, a program).

text processing This is a somewhat vague term with two different meanings. Sometimes it's a synonym for **formatting**, with many stand-alone formatters calling themselves **text processors;** other times it's a generic term that covers **word processing, mailing list programs, spelling checkers** and all similar software.

thermal printer A printer that uses heat to form characters on special paper.

thimble The **print element** used on NEC Spinwriter **formed-character printers.** It's like a **daisy wheel** with the stalks bent up into a cup shape, and works in the same basic manner.

thin-window display A non-CRT display that shows just one line, or part of a line. Typically, it runs across the top of a keyboard.

third generation Computers that use integrated circuits (chips) for their switches. (Some people refer to these as fourth-generation computers and call the third-generation computers ones that use transistors for their switches.) See the chart at **fourth generation.**

360 See **IBM 360.**

3740 format See **IBM 3740 format.**

Thomas J. Watson Research Center See under **Watson.**

thx See **tnx.**

time sharing Sharing the use of a large computer you don't own with many other users. You're billed (usually monthly) on the basis of your **connect time**—the exact amount of time you're connected to the system.

tnx or **thx** {hacker jargon} An abbreviation for "thanks"—widely used to save time and effort in typed conversations on computer terminals.

Tnx 10E6 means "thanks a million." 10E6 is a way of writing 10^6 when you can't display superscripts (the E stands for "exponent"); 10^6 is, of course, ten to the sixth power, or one million.

toggle Any command that switches back and forth between two possible alternatives (insert mode and writeover mode, for example). Also used as a verb.

(to) tool {hacker jargon} To work or study. Hacker X: *Want to play a little space war?* Hacker Y: *No, thanks. Got to tool.*

track Data is stored on disks in concentric tracks (sort of like the grooves on a phonograph record, but not connected with each other). A typical 8" floppy contains 77 tracks, each of which is divided into several **sectors.**

trackball A spherical device, mounted on some keyboards, used to control the movement of the cursor. You may be familiar with it from the popular arcade football game where the players are moved by spinning a similar device. Also see **CAT, mouse** and **rotary control knob.**

tractor feed A lightweight, mechanically simple paper-feeding device that attaches to the top of a printer and engages sprocket holes in the paper with pins. The distance between the pins can be altered to accommodate papers of different widths. Compare **pin feed** and **friction feed.**

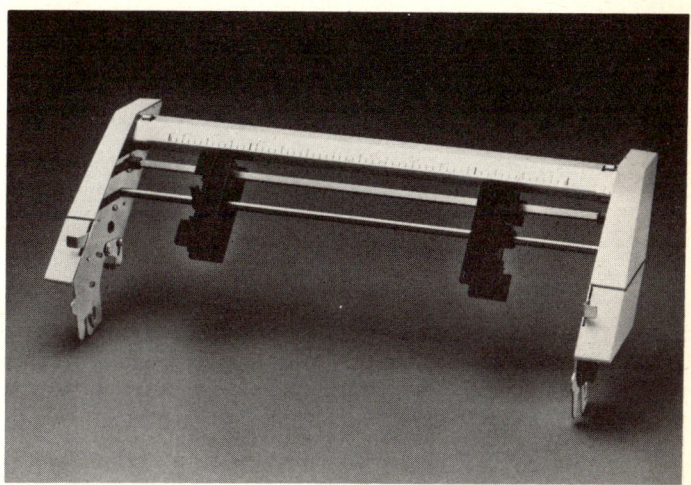

a tractor feed   COURTESY OF QUME CORPORATION—A SUBSIDIARY OF ITT

training manual A manual designed to be used while a program (or complete system) is being learned. Also called a **tutorial.** Compare **reference manual.**

TRSDOS (TRISS-doss) Radio Shack's **operating system** for its TRS-80 computers. The name is short for "Tandy-Radio Shack disk operating system."

TTY An abbreviation for a *tele*t*y*pewriter-like **terminal** or, sometimes, for any kind of terminal at all.

Turing, Alan M. (1912–54) British mathematician and logician who devised the **Turing test** and set forth many of the basic concepts on which all computer design is based.

Turing test A method devised by Alan M. Turing to decide whether what a computer does can be called thinking. In one room you put a group of people (the testers); in another room you put the testee, which is either a computer or a person—the testers don't know which. In each room is a terminal, and they're connected to each other. The testers and the testee then carry on a conversation.

If the testers can't decide if they're talking to a person or a computer (and they are in fact talking to a computer), then the computer is obviously capable of thinking (since what it's doing is indistinguishable from what we call "thinking" when a person does it).

Turing test   GAR SMITH

No computer in existence today can even dream of passing the Turing test—but then again, neither can most newscasters, corporate executives or four-star generals.

turtle graphics The ability to draw lines and shapes on the screen by telling the **cursor** how far you want to move and in what direction, rather than by having to provide coordinates—that is, you can say *turn 30° left and go three inches*, rather than having to say *draw a line from x240 y170 to x380 y520*. Turtle graphics are used in **LOGO** and some other programming languages.

What, you may ask, does all this have to do with turtles? Well, mechanical turtles that draw lines on paper are often used to teach the basic principles of LOGO turtle graphics to children. When the kids advance to drawing on the screen, they're told to think of the cursor as a turtle painting lines with its tail.

tutorial Another name for a **training manual**. (Be aware that in the world of computers, "tutorial" usually means a book or a program, not a class.)

(to) tweak {hacker jargon} To change slightly; to fine-tune. Compare **frobnicate** and **twiddle**.

24 x 80 (the x is pronounced "by") Twenty-four lines of eighty characters—the most common format for displaying text on a computer screen. Sometimes there's a 25th "status" line which can't be used for text but tells you things like where you are in a file or whether you're in insert or writeover mode. Compare **16 x 64**.

(to) twiddle {hacker jargon} To change something slightly, but not as slightly as when you **tweak** it. See **frobnicate** for more on the distinction.

A **twiddle** is a small and insignificant change made to a program.

type See **file type**.
   TYPE is a command in CP/M and PC DOS that displays the contents of a file on the screen (or feeds it to a printer).

type-ahead buffer A **buffer** that remembers which keys were struck when the computer—for one reason or another—is busy doing something else and can't pay attention to them.

.TXT (dot-TEE-ex-TEE, or dot-TEXT) A common **file type** for

text files. It's short for "text" (of course). **.DOC** (for "document") is also used. Compare **.COM**.

U

u A common abbreviation for **micron** or **micro-** (in the sense of one-millionth), because the lowercase Greek letter mu (μ), which is the *real* abbreviation, looks a lot like a lowercase u. (Comes the revolution, we'll all have Greek character sets on our word processors and this tawdry pretense will no longer be necessary.)

UCSD Pascal A popular variety of the **Pascal** programming language, developed at the University of California's San Diego campus.

UCSD p-System An **operating system** developed at the University of California's San Diego campus. The p-System is usually sold with an integral programming language like Pascal or FORTRAN. The "p" stands for "pseudo-code" (don't worry about what that means).

unbundled Sold separately, rather than all in one package. If a system is unbundled, you can buy just the parts of it you want, filling in the missing components with your own selections bought elsewhere. As opposed to **bundled**.

undo A very useful command in some word processing programs that undoes the effect of the last command (or series of commands) and puts your text back the way it was.

UNIVAC (YOU-ni-vac) The first electronic digital computer to be sold commercially (by Remington Rand in 1950). It was developed by J. Presper Eckert, Jr., and John Mauchly, who had earlier built **ENIAC**. A total of 48 UNIVACs were manufactured.

UNIX (YOU-nix) A common **operating system** for sixteen-bit (and larger) machines, developed at Bell Labs.

up Working (as opposed to **down**).

(to) update To incorporate changes. (The word is a little misleading, since the up*date* usually occurs just a fraction of a second after the changes, not a day or two.) *The screen isn't updated until thirty to forty milliseconds after you press the key.*

(to) upload To transfer data from a nearby computer to a distant computer. Compare **download**.

us (or, more properly, μs) Abbreviation for **microsecond**.

user Someone who uses programs written by other people, rather than writing her or his own. As opposed to a **programmer**.

In **hacker** jargon, the word usually has the connotation of "pitiful mindless scum." *Well of course he doesn't understand what you're talking about; he's a user.* Hackers tend to call users **losers** or—just to make the point really clear—**lusers**.

"User" is also used generically, to mean anybody who works on a computer, whether s/he programs it or not. *They've crammed 750 users onto a machine designed to handle 40.*

user group A club made up of people who use (or who are interested in) a particular piece of hardware or software. ("User" is a general term here and doesn't necessarily mean "nonprogrammer.")

User groups are typically independent of (not affiliated with) the company that makes the product. Most large cities have user groups for many major brands of microcomputers and sometimes also for popular programs like VisiCalc. User groups are great places to get information, since their members are (usually) not trying to sell you anything and often know more than the sales clerks in computer stores (which isn't saying much).

user interface How a piece of hardware or software appears to the people who use it; what the product is like to work with. *Xerox PARC developed the user interface that features the mouse and "icons" (little pictures on the screen).*

user memory Another name for **RAM**.

user-friendly Said of a piece of software or hardware, this means you don't need a Ph.D. in Computer Science to understand how to use it. Also called **friendly**.

utility Either of two properties—Electric Company and Water Works—that it's particularly useful to own early in the game.

Also, a **utility program**—a type of **systems software** that performs a relatively simple task like listing the names of all the files on a disk, copying a file, copying a whole disk, or sorting a list of **records**. Many people put a few basic utilities on every disk they use.

V

value I hate these words that are so general it's almost impossible to define them. A value is what you set a **parameter** to. Well, that was easy.

All right, all right—let's say you have a word processing program that lets you change the margins (and if you have one that doesn't, get another one). The number of spaces you want between the first letter on each line and the left edge of the paper is the value you set the parameter called "left margin" to. If you try to set the left margin at 527 spaces, the program might come back at you with the following question: "VALUE?"

This does not mean—as well it might—"what is the value of putting your left margin 527 spaces from the left edge of the paper?" Rather it means: "what kind of cockamamie value is 527 for 'left margin'? My programmer told me never to accept a value of more than 60 for this parameter."

Values are usually numbers, but they don't have to be. For example, *on* can be a value for page numbering (as opposed to *off*); *b* can be a value for justification (meaning "justify to both margins," as opposed to *l*—"justify to the left margin only").

vanilla {hacker jargon} Standard; ordinary. *This is an absolutely vanilla interface; you can buy the hardware for it at any electronics store in the world.*

As the Jargon File points out, the hacker meaning and the normal meaning (or should I say the vanilla meaning?) for vanilla can conflict when you talk about food. For example, to say you want "vanilla wonton soup" doesn't mean you'd like the cook to put vanilla in it; it means you want regular wonton soup, not wor wonton soup or some other special kind.

VAX (vaks) A **DEC** computer which is technically a **minicomputer** but is more powerful than some **mainframes** (and for that reason is sometimes called a *maxicomputer*). The name stands for "*v*irtual *a*ddress e*x*tension." The hacker jargon plural is **VAXen,** in imitation of "oxen."

VDT A "video display terminal"—i.e., a keyboard and CRT combination, capable of communicating with a computer. As distinguished from a **printer terminal.**

VDU A "visual display unit"—the British name for a VDT.

vendor The company (or person) that sells you something (as distinguished from the manufacturer or publisher that makes it).

verification (of a save) A process where a program goes back after a file has been saved and makes a character-by-character comparison of what's on disk with what's in memory, looking for discrepancies caused by **glitches** or other malfunctions.

versions (of programs) Progressive refinements and enhancements, numbered in ascending order. Versions are almost always given as decimal numbers, with 1.0 typically being the first **release version.** Version 2.0 indicates a more major revision of Version 1.0 than, say, Version 1.7.

very-large-scale integration See **VLSI.**

video board In **memory-mapped** mode, the **board** which plugs into the computer **box** and controls the display on a monitor. Together with a CRT and a keyboard, it substitutes for a terminal.

video (display) terminal A VDT.

visual editor A screen editor.

virtual {hacker jargon} Performing the functions of; acting like. *The system of swapping the workfile on and off disk is sometimes called virtual memory, because it seems like the whole file is in memory even though it isn't* (actually, it doesn't really seem that way at all, but the term "virtual memory" is still applied to it). Also see **logical**.

VLSI "Very-large-scale integration"—**integrated circuit** technology that allows the equivalent of more than 50,000 transistors to be crammed onto a single chip. See the chart at **chip**.

von Neumann, John (1903–57) Hungarian-born mathematical genius and polymath (if you have to look it up, you're not one). Among many other things, von Neumann was a pioneer in the design and development of computers. Working at the Institute for Advanced Study at Princeton University, he and Herman Goldstine built one of the first computers.

vulture capitalists {hacker jargon} A nickname for venture capitalists—who, in addition to providing many small companies with needed capital, sometimes also suck them dry and toss their husks onto the dust heap of history.

#

warm boot Another name for a **reboot**.

Watson, Thomas J., Sr. (1874–1956) Industrialist who joined the Computing-Tabulating-Recording Company in 1914 and over the next forty years forged it into a transnational behemoth called IBM.

T.J. Watson, Sr. (1874–1956).
COURTESY OF INTERNATIONAL BUSINESS MACHINES CORPORATION

Watson, Thomas J., Jr. (1914–) Son of IBM's founder who rescued the company from its late start in computers and guided it to the point where nine out of ten people taking a word-association test would probably respond "IBM" if you said "computer."

Thomas J. **Watson Research Center** IBM's in-house computer think tank in Yorktown Heights, New York.

wedged {hacker jargon} Another name for **catatonic**—i.e., locked up, stuck. Sometimes due to a **deadlock.**

the **West Coast Computer Faire** The preeminent convention for microcomputer users (as opposed to dealers, manufacturers and distributors); many new products are introduced there each year. It's held every March or so in San Francisco and, by the time you read this, it will be drawing close to 50,000 people (which, given the limited floor space, makes it a frotteur's paradise).

what {hacker jargon} A spoken abbreviation for "question mark." Useful when proofreading: *Quote tennis comma anyone what endquote burbled the preppie period.*

widow The last line of a paragraph sitting alone at the top of a page of text. Also, a single word ending a paragraph and thus sitting on a line by itself. Some word processing programs know how to suppress (the first kind of) widows. Also see **orphan**.

Wiener, Norbert (1894–1964) Mathematician and author of a pioneering work on computers, *Cybernetics: Or Control and Communication in the Animal and the Machine* (1948). He also wrote *The Human Use of Human Beings* (1950).

wildcard A symbol which means "any character" or "any sequence of characters" (just as a wild card in poker stands for any card). For example, * is a wildcard in **CP/M, PC DOS** and some other **operating systems.** If you ask for a **directory** of *.TXT, you'll get a list of every file with the **file type** .TXT; if you ask for a directory of b*.*, you'll get a list of every file whose name starts with the letter b, regardless of the file type.

(to) win {hacker jargon} To succeed. **Winner** can refer to a person or a thing. *Of course it's a winner; all my programs win.* **Real winner** is also widely used—sometimes sarcastically. **Winning** is the adjective.

A **win** is something which succeeds. *What a moby win that idea was!* The result of success, the benefit obtained, is called **winnage** (WIN-ij). The ability to succeed, being successful, is called **winnitude.** Hacker X: *We corrected that lossage last week and it's been solid winnage since then.* Hacker Y: *That's great! What winnitude!*

Compare **lose**, etc. See **bogus** for a list of antonyms.

Winchester A relatively inexpensive kind of **fixed hard disk drive** that features very light read/write heads positioned very close to the disk. The disk is sealed in a dust-free enclosure. Despite a number of more colorful stories, the name comes from Winchester Boulevard in San Jose, California, where the IBM facility that first developed Winchesters was located.

window The portion of a file that appears on the screen at any given time. If the program you're using has a **split-screen** feature, more than one window can be displayed at one time.

wizard {hacker jargon} A hacker who really knows his or her stuff. *What do you mean, how long will it take me to debug it? I'm a wizard—my programs don't have bugs.*

word "Word" has a technical, computer meaning (which you can ignore) and also a traditional meaning in typing—four letters and a space. There's only one problem with this: words do not, in fact, average four letters. In my own writing they average closer to five—six with the space. (I know this because my word processing program gives me the length of each file in both **K** and words, so all I have to do is divide.)

Since I'm not fond of fancy, sesquipedalian words (except for that one), it's not likely that my words are longer—on the average—than most people's (if anything, they're shorter).

1K contains 205 official (nonexistent) typing words, 170 actual words. If a printer does 55 **cps,** it prints about 550 (real) words per minute. (True wpm is ten times cps, but cps is 1/12th of wpm—because they use imaginary five-character words when they quote wpm in an ad.)

word processing Using a computer to write, edit and format text.

word processing program Software that tells a computer how to accept, edit and format text.

word processor A computer set up to accept, edit, format and print out text. There are two main types: **dedicated word processors,** and general-purpose computers running word processing programs.

Sometimes a **word processing program** all by itself is referred to as a word processor.

word wrap A feature that automatically moves a word, all in one piece, to the beginning of the next line if there isn't room for it at the end of the line it started out on.

work-alike A piece of hardware that imitates hardware made by another company so closely that they both will run all the same software. Typically the work-alike offers all the features of the original and then some. One example is the Franklin Ace, which is a work-alike of the Apple II but has several enhancements. Compare **look-alike.**

work disk A disk you alter, as opposed to a **master disk.**
Also—particularly on systems with small disk capaci-

ties—a disk with **data files** on it, as opposed to a **system disk**, which has programs (like the operating system and word processing program) on it.

workfile The file currently in memory and being worked on.

workspace The portion of memory set aside for you to put your text (or other data) into.

work station A chair, desk, terminal, etc.—the place where one person works. This is mostly a business term; you wouldn't refer to the place where you use a home computer as your "work station" (except whimsically).

wow {hacker jargon} A spoken abbreviation for "exclamation mark." **Bang** and **excl** are also used.

WP Abbreviation for **word processing.**

wpm "Words per minute." See **word** for more about this.

write To deposit information on a disk or other storage medium. Compare **read**.

write-protect slot On some **floppy disks,** this prevents the disk from being **written** to unless it's covered over with a small sticker; on others, it prevents the disk from being written to *if* it's covered over. In either case, it serves to protect important data from accidental erasure.

writeover mode When a word processing program is in this mode, it replaces characters that are already on the screen with ones you type. Opposite of **insert mode.**

X

x-axis On a graph, chart or any sort of rectilinear grid, the horizontal direction. Time is usually put on the x-axis. Compare **y-axis.**

XENIX (zee-nix) A **look-alike** of the **UNIX operating system** that runs on microcomputers. Developed by Microsoft.

Xerox PARC (zeer-ox park) Xerox Corporation's Palo Alto Research Center in Silicon Valley. PARC pioneered work on the **mouse** and other **user-friendly** features which have since been implemented in the Xerox 8010 Star and the Apple Lisa. The **Smalltalk** programming language was also developed at Xerox PARC.

Y

y-axis On a graph, chart or any sort of rectilinear grid, the vertical direction. Quantity is usually put on the y-axis. Compare **x-axis**.

yo-yo mode {hacker jargon} A system is in this state when it alternates between being up and being down several times during a short period. The term can also be applied to people: *Whenever he gets this close to a deadline, he goes into yo-yo mode. You never know from one day to the next if he's going to be really together or a total space case.*

Z

Z80 One of the most common **eight-bit chips,** made by Zilog—designed to be an upgrade of Intel's 8080 chip. (Later versions are called the **Z80A** and the **Z80B**.)

Computer Dictionary for Beginners

Z8000 A **sixteen-bit chip** made by Zilog.

zoom video A feature that lets you magnify a portion of the text on the screen. It's usually found on full-page screens, where the normal text is rather small.

\ (called a **backslash**) A special symbol found on most computer keyboards, often used to distinguish **embedded** commands from text in the middle of a line (where a **dot command** can't be placed).

/\/\/\ {hacker jargon} When conversing on computer terminals, this is the written equivalent of a giggle.

* (called a **star** much more often than an asterisk; also called a **splat** or a **glob**) In **CP/M, PC DOS** and some other **operating systems,** * is a **wildcard** that stands for "any sequence of characters."

  * is commonly used in computer programming to indicate multiplication. Thus 2*2 = 2 × 2.

? In **CP/M, PC DOS** and some other **operating systems,** the question mark is a **wildcard** that stands for "any single character."

. (called a **dot,** not a period) In **CP/M, PC DOS, FLEX** and some other **operating systems,** the divider between a **file name** and a **file type.** Also see **dot command.** Terms beginning with a dot (like .TXT and .BAK) are listed above under their first letter.

: In **CP/M, PC DOS** and some other **operating systems,** the colon is used after a letter to indicate "disk drive." Thus A: means "drive A," B: means "drive B," and so on.

ABOUT THE AUTHOR

In addition to this book, Arthur Naiman is the author of *Every Goy's Guide to Common Jewish Expressions*, *Word Processing Buyer's Guide*, *The First Book to Read about the IBM Personal Computer* and *Introduction to WordStar*. He is at work on several more books, both about computers and on other subjects.